CHOOSE
TO WIN

CHOOSE TO WIN

SUSIE O'NEILL

NEW EDITION

ACHIEVING YOUR GOALS, FULFILLING YOUR DREAMS

WITH FIONA CHAPPELL

MACMILLAN
Pan Macmillan Australia

To Mum, Dad, John and Catherine,
For their love, encouragement and values.

To Cliff,
For keeping me laughing.

To Scott and Mr Wakefield,
Without whom my victories would not have been possible.

First published 1998 in Macmillan by Pan Macmillan Australia Pty Limited,
St Martins Tower, 31 Market Street, Sydney

Revised and updated 1999

Copyright © Susie O'Neill 1998

National Library of Australia
cataloguing-in-publication data:

O'Neill, Susie.
Choose to win.

Rev. ed.
ISBN 0 7329 0995 3.

1. O'Neill, Susie, 1973– . 2. Success–Handbooks, manuals, etc.
3. Goal (Psychology)–Handbooks, manuals, etc.
4. Swimming–Training–Psychological aspects. I. Title.

158.1

Typeset in 11/15 Garamond by Post Pre-Press Group
Printed in Australia by McPherson's Printing Group

Acknowledgements

Several people have participated in the preparation of this book. Special thanks must go to Scott Volkers, Don Talbot, Bernie Wakefield, Elli Overton, Michael Bohl, the O'Neill family, Rob Woodhouse and the staff at Queensland Swimming who contributed their time and insight.

I would also like to thank the *Courier-Mail* sports editors Gary Smart and Neil Breen, for their understanding in allowing me time off at short notice, and Mike Colman, Robert Craddock, Paul Malone and Jim Fagan for their wonderful advice and interest. Plus Tom Gilliatt and my editor Alexandra Mohan, for their help and guidance.

Finally I must thank Chris for his wit, his belief in me and his incredible support. Thanks to Mum, Dad, Alison and Kirsty for their encouragement and love and most of all Susie, for giving me the opportunity to be a part of this rewarding experience and for her honesty and courage in sharing her life.

Fiona Chappell

Fiona Chappell won an academic scholarship to the St Catherine's Anglican Girls school in Sydney and graduated from the Queensland University of Technology with a Bachelor of Business degree in journalism. She started in newspapers in 1987 and has contributed to numerous magazine and newspaper publications. Fiona has won several awards for her coverage of sport for the *Courier-Mail* in Brisbane and has covered Wimbledon, the Indy 500, the World Gymnastic and Softball Championships and the Hockey World Cup. She is active in getting recognition for sportswomen as a member of the Queensland Womensport Association.

CONTENTS

BY SHANE GOULD

It is usually from older people that we seek life's wisdom and answers. Occasionally, though, a young sage presents herself with insights into life that are far beyond her years of living experience. Susie O'Neill is one of those 'wise ones' and she shares her knowings with us in this book *Choose To Win*. I am a student of her wisdom.

Susie has all the elements of the formula for success, T.S.T.L.: Talent (you're born with), Skills (you can develop), Try (heart and desire), and Luck (spelt w-o-r-k, and defined as 'where preparation meets opportunity').

Her success, though, is not only in the fantastic results of her Olympic Medals, but even more importantly, in the person she has become in the process. The challenges she has dealt with in her long swimming career have developed endurance and character. Susie evokes hope both for herself and for the others who will come after her. Hope draws us to the future; a future where top-level sport is a fine direction for our children to take because it is played fairly and cleanly.

There are many who are critical of participation in elite sport. Susie is a fine example of the positive benefits it provides. Currently there is despair about drugs in sport; sport being degraded and young athletic bodies being damaged. But Susie demonstrates that success can be achieved without drugs, and she knows that her mighty effort alone has made her a winner. This confidence in her ability will always be with her, and we all know that her story isn't finished yet.

Susie O'Neill, you're a worthy member of the Gold Medal Club.

Shane Gould, Margaret River – Western Australia

1

PART ONE

Diving into the deep
Birth to 1994

Sink or swim. There comes a time when everyone has a choice of giving up or persevering and making it work. These were my options by the end of 1994.

Only a small percentage of people are born with natural confidence and I was never one of that rare breed. I immediately took to swimming but not so to competition. For some unknown reason I would panic halfway through a race and become so gripped by fear that I didn't believe I could reach the other end of the pool. This happened for years, but I eventually overcame it. Then, when I did start to show some promise, I would secretly dread being chosen for teams because I was extremely shy among people I didn't know. Self-doubt was stopping me from being the swimmer I had the potential to be.

Then came the external threats: the drug-driven Chinese and the public expectations. All these factors fed my self-doubt and so by 1994 I felt I was slowly sinking and retirement was staring me in the face. All I had going for me was a determination to not only survive but to win.

1

PAIN

'Anyone can stand tall on the high peaks. It is the people who survive the valleys between the peaks who will emerge the strongest.'
PRESTON PEARSON

'I realise success is having the courage to meet failure without being defeated.'
PHIL NIEKRO

'What is defeat? Nothing but education; nothing but the first step to something better.' **WENDELL PHILLIPS**

I **negotiated a turn, then another and then slammed on the brakes for a red light.** I was driving to the 1994 Commonwealth Games trials in Brisbane. This was a route I drove twice daily to training at the Chandler Aquatic Centre. I had become familiar with every turn and every traffic light. But today was different. I was competing, and I carried a heavy weight on my shoulders. I had a sudden urge to keep driving past the Chandler turn-off and not stop until I was as far away from the trials as I could be.

At that moment everything seemed too hard. In fact, I wanted to be free from swimming altogether. Anything was better than having to compete. I had become depressed about my career because nothing seemed to be going right. I knew I was going to swim badly and I was scared of failure in the very public forum of the Commonwealth Games trials.

It wasn't the first time such negative thoughts had entered my head. I suppose I was looking for the perfect excuse to escape from swimming because, sadly, I was no longer enjoying the sport. So much so that I could no longer see a future in swimming. It was as though I was going through the motions while I waited for something better to come along.

People say you cannot be successful until you learn to like yourself but on that day I was so miserable it seemed impossible to feel happy about myself let alone my swimming. Looking back, I can't believe I felt so depressed about swimming. Now it seems logical to have taken a step back and analysed why I was so frustrated but at the time I was incapable of doing that. By 1994, swimming ruled my life and every failure came as a bitter blow.

In the car that day and before all my races I had this awful sickly feeling. My nerves were uncontrollable. I had lost my confidence after a time trial the day before the trials. I knew then I was not going to have a good meet. I felt lethargic and heavy in the water and my arms felt weak and brittle, as though they were twigs. Something I called 'twiggy'. I was trying hard but it felt like I was going backwards.

The trials were a real shock. I knew I was swimming badly and the writing was on the wall, and I knew I had to get stuck into training. But I had no motivation. I just remember counting the days between the trials and the Games because I couldn't wait for the competition to be over. In fact, in 1994 I constantly thought about retiring. I remember having a lot of private cries that year as I searched for answers. By the time I reached the Games I had lost all excitement and enjoyment for swimming.

There were a lot of days when I felt really down. All I did that year was swim and I had no outside interest because, without realising it, I had cut myself off from any social life. I wasn't mixing much with people. I was just training, eating and sleeping. Looking back, this factor probably contributed to my swimming low.

I've always over-analysed things and when you have a lot of time to think about your problems, they seem to double in size. I was haunted by the biggest fear of every athlete: I had reached my peak. I had come to believe I was never going to swim faster. I had not improved from the end of 1992 to the end of 1994 in my main event, the 200m butterfly, and I felt I was going backwards.

I knew I had some tough decisions to make about my future, especially whether to keep swimming. It was a draining and upsetting time. I felt I couldn't go forward until I had decided on my future. In every event I carried the weight this could be one of my last races. I was swimming for my career.

LEARNING FROM A CAREER LOW

Everybody experiences highs and lows. I suppose to gain the exhilaration and satisfaction of reaching the peaks you have to start climbing from a point lower down. More importantly, you learn more about yourself when things go wrong than when you experience the heights of success. That is why it is important to analyse your valleys and to learn to map your upward climbs, to help you with the directions to your next peak. But nothing prepared me for my biggest low – the 1994 Commonwealth Games in Victoria, Canada.

Up until then my career had sailed along and hard work had helped me to achieve my goals and conquer minor hurdles. I had yet to strike a long-term barrier. When it came, I had no idea how to handle it and what was to blame. Now I realise adversity was probably the best thing that could have happened to me, because it made me stop and rethink my direction.

I will always remember 1994 as the year I swam badly and experienced a terrible low. I was billed as a swimmer who could win seven gold medals at the Commonwealth Games but instead, with low confidence and little motivation, I bombed out in several events in which I started as favourite.

Despite the painful memories, the Games proved to be the turning point in my career. Afterwards I thoroughly examined my swimming career and whether I should retire. I gained courage from my failures in 1994, enough to analyse my direction and consider changes. I realised I could no longer sit back and let things stay the same if I wanted to jump to the next peak.

On my return home I sat down and listed what went wrong. It was one of the best things I could have done, because it gave me a written record of my disappointments. It is amazing how when you see your problems written down you gain a clearer picture of what has gone wrong, plus the problems do not seem so overwhelming because they are confined to a sheet of paper.

I was able not only to visualise my problems but also the solutions. Seeing my past mistakes on paper helped me to realise the traps I had fallen prey to in 1994. When I was feeling down in 1994 my bad form was such a mystery, but looking back there were several warning signs I can't believe I failed to recognise. It takes a lot of courage to dissect and analyse bad memories but the exercise is usually rewarded. By examining what went wrong, I understood what I needed to do to achieve my goal of winning an Olympic gold medal. More importantly, it became my first step towards something better. Here is what I discovered in my search for answers.

A STEP-BY-STEP ANALYSIS OF WHAT WENT WRONG

Burnt out

When you are reaching for the stars and enjoying the hard work, challenges and rewards along the way, it is easy to become burnt out. You are so intent on striving for future dreams you are not looking after the realities of the present, such as making sure you keep things in perspective.

In 1992, all I did was swim. I loved swimming and it was exciting to see all my hard work paying off. Looking back I was probably too full-on but at the time I was oblivious of the dangers.

Then I was on a high after winning the bronze medal at the 1992 Barcelona Olympics. I missed out on winning a gold medal by 0.36 of a second. Gold seemed so close and I was keen to start my campaign as soon as possible. I didn't suffer the usual post-Olympic letdown, when athletes experience a low after working and focusing so hard on peaking for their Olympic goal. Instead, my enthusiasm was at its highest. In hindsight, I needed a mental and physical break after the most intensive campaign of my career so far. It is a very human need to 'chill-out' and slow down after a hectic schedule and go fishing, relax on the beach or whatever as long as it takes you as far away from work as possible. Timely rest is a crucial part of success. It's important to take your rest when you can and I should have done so before the next serious meetings, the 1994 Commonwealth Games and 1994 World Championships.

But at that time I didn't know about pacing myself and I leapt straight back into training and racing. I just raced, raced and raced and believed everything was rosy. 1993 was a really hectic racing year and I went on five overseas campaigns as well as a sprint camp in Hawaii. I was learning so much from racing some of the world's best and having so much fun, that the burnout factor crept up on me. Suddenly, by the end of 1993, I was drained, restless from all the travelling, really sick of racing and had become blasé about competitions.

Now I make sure I have a proper break, especially after major competitions and the intensive training sessions leading to them. It is important to live a whole and balanced life, particularly during the times when you don't have the pressure of intense competition.

Superficial high

There are two kinds of success. There is the success which comes from hard work and a solid build-up and success which seems strong on the outside but is hollow because it has no foundation. I liken it to a superficial high, and this is what I experienced in 1993.

In early 1993 I struck major success at the World Cup circuit in Europe with meets in France, Germany, England and Sweden. It was written up as the best series of international performances by an Australian swimmer since Shane Gould in 1972. I won 12 World Cup races, setting eight national short course records in the process. My short course 100m butterfly time, 59.47 seconds, was the fourth fastest all-time in the world.

But it was only a superficial high. On the surface everything looked great and I was continuing on from my bronze medal success at Barcelona. I was travelling around Europe, was highly competitive at all the meets and having a lot of fun. But really I was heading for a fall. My main focus since Barcelona had been to race instead of building a solid training base. This helped to keep me race-fit but I had no training foundation, which you need for every major competition. You cannot expect to succeed when you have not completed your training.

At the time I didn't realise this. I thought everything was on track. The World Cup success had put my expectations off balance. A lot of my competitors were probably training through the racing while I was rested. The year after the Olympics the competition is traditionally the least testing, because many of the big stars are not at full strength after taking post-Olympic breaks. After my barnstorming campaign in February 1993, I thought I was further ahead than I really was.

I continued my successful run the following month at the 1993 National Championships held in Perth, not realising it was my training base from 1992 that was the foundation of my form. I swam a personal best in the 200m freestyle and won the 100m and 200m doubles in both butterfly and freestyle.

Australian Institute of Sport coach Gennadi Touretski, who coached Russian Alex Popov to dual 50m and 100m Olympic titles, invited me on the institute's tour of Europe in May and June. It was a big honour and I never dreamed of turning it down. We had competitions in France and Spain and then a trip to New Zealand followed in July where again I continued to set fast times.

By the Pan Pacs in August I was jaded, but at the same time success had seemed to come pretty easily that year. I didn't see the danger in the lack of quality training. I had forgotten how hard I had to work. I didn't train nearly as much as I usually did. My coach Mr Wakefield never had a chance to work with me because I was away on so many camps and overseas tours. I was having fun and getting plenty of race practice, but this doesn't mean anything when you have no training base to fall back on.

High expectations

With success comes expectation and expectation always brings a new set of challenges. Once people expect you to do well, new pressures and new situations arise. Other people will look at you in a new light but it is important you never see yourself differently. When expectations become public then they are always harder to overcome but the key is to keep your private expectations at an achievable level.

It is not surprising my overseas success had gathered some high expectations. For the first time with my swimming, people were not predicting success but were expecting it. By February 1993 the media was writing about me achieving an unprecedented seven gold medals at the 1994 Commonwealth Games. My coach Mr Wakefield was also quoted as saying this. (Because I began training with him when I was very young, I have always called my coach Bernie Wakefield 'Mr Wakefield'.) Kieren Perkins was quoted as saying I should start to think like a world-beater to break world records. Then also during this time there were some stories saying I was the next Shane Gould or Dawn Fraser. Suddenly, with all this expectation, I felt a bit of pressure.

Mr Wakefield regularly linked my name with Shane and Dawn. It was flattering and I suppose he wanted to give me some motivation but I would have preferred if he had not publicly predicted things before they happened, just in case they never happened.

It's very hard when you are compared to people in the past like Dawn and Shane. It's hard because you've never competed against them and they belong in a different era and swam under different circumstances. It's flattering to be compared to such swimmers I highly respect but it also means there's a lot of expectation. I haven't won a gold medal in the same event in three consecutive Olympics like Dawn, or held every world record from 100m to 1500m and won three gold medals at the same Olympics like Shane.

At the beginning I could not help but be conscious of this new expectation. And the expectation of being the next Dawn Fraser or Shane Gould can become a terrible burden to carry into a race. Now I believe the less attention you pay to public expectation and the more you concentrate on yourself and your goals, the better chance of continued success.

More importantly, I am Susie O'Neill and no other person. I chase my own goals and have always aimed to be my own person. I set my own pace and follow no-one else's. I learnt to know what level I am at and what I am capable of, and that has become my expectation.

Complacency

When you achieve success easily you don't have the reminder of hard work, so it is only natural that complacency can set in. Complacency can take over from success if you let it.

Success came all too easily for me in early 1993: I was swimming fast in every meet and my confidence was high. But it was a superficial high and I had an unrealistic view of my form. It was not surprising then that I had a fall at the 1993 Pan Pacs in Japan.

The Pan Pacs are the only meet when the 200m butterfly is on the first day. Only two Australians are allowed through to the final. Mr Wakefield and the media were talking about world record attempts on the 200m butterfly and this was the hot topic on the eve of the Pan Pacs. I was favourite for the 200m butterfly and carried the world's number one ranking into the race after my early 1993 success. Looking back, I suppose I just expected to sail straight into the final.

We had the 200m freestyle and the 200 butterfly on the same night. I swam terribly in the 200m freestyle but I managed to get through to the final. Then I had the 200m butterfly almost straight away. All three Australians were in the same heat. Julie Majer, Petria Thomas and myself were all together with one lap remaining in the race and in the past I had been able to swim away from them.

I remember hurting so much in that last lap. My strokes were short and laboured. I finished third fastest qualifier behind Majer and Thomas and missed the final in a time that was more than three seconds slower than my bronze medal race at Barcelona the year before.

It was devastating. And it was the first time I cried over a race, something I never thought I would do. I remember thinking when I was younger, 'Imagine crying over a swimming race!' I had seen other competitors cry publicly after races but I had never wanted to show my emotions with such public exhibitions. I suppose I came from a family that believed in the old saying about actions speaking louder than words. I showed people how I felt through my swimming, not in my reactions and interviews after races.

This time things were different and I did cry, but only in private. This was probably the worst failure of my career and I really felt it. When I was younger it was all fun and I had no great expectations. But I came into the race after a successful season when I won everything with ease, and then could not even make the Pan Pac final in the event in which I won the Olympic bronze medal.

There were some factors that could excuse my performance. I had a stomach upset and I had the 'twiggy' heavy feeling in the water, which made it likely my competition taper was out. But really it came down to not being mentally prepared. I had become complacent because I didn't think the other Australians could really beat me.

I used my 200m butterfly failure as motivation for the rest of the competition. This tactic worked. I came back the next day and set personal bests and Commonwealth records in the heat and final of the 100m freestyle to win a silver medal. The following day I won the silver medal in the 100m butterfly.

After that meet I vowed never to be complacent again. I had always considered the 1993 Pan Pacs as a disaster but now I realise I did have a pretty good competition because I was able to recover from the disappointment of the first day and swim a couple of best times. Most importantly, I had learnt the hard way about how easy it was to be complacent and I have never fallen into that trap again.

Plateau

The biggest fear for anyone is they have reached their peak, that they are past improvement. You cannot win without mental strength and believing you are never going to improve would have to be the hardest mental handicap to overcome.

At the end of 1993 I started to be plagued by such doubts, which gained force at the 1993 World Short Course Championships held in Majorca in December. I won four silver medals but saved my best performance until the end when I won gold on the last day. I recorded 59.19 in the 100m butterfly to beat Chinese rival Limin Liu.

At the time I didn't realise the significance of the victory. I wasn't to know it would take another two years to record my next win against the Chinese, who were rumoured to be powered by drugs. I was so consumed by negative thoughts about my own swimming that the historic win could not dislodge the doubts.

I believe it was at these championships that I started to lose my momentum with swimming. I could not help but wonder if I was on my way down. It is not surprising then that in 1994 I came to believe I had reached my peak. I was hovering on my first long-term plateau, I felt stale and had many doubts I could ever go faster. I kept thinking, 'Maybe this is as good as I will get.'

There is a theory that athletes only reach plateaus when they forget how hard they have to work to improve. I was probably guilty of that. I had enjoyed tremendous success in early 1993 without realising I was riding on the work of the past years. The plateau came when there was a lot of expectation I would reach that next level. As well as a faltering work ethic I also lacked the belief I could improve.

I knew the key was to regain my hunger and believe I could soar to the next peak.

Ruled by work

Obviously it is important to have a commitment to work but it is equally important not to go overboard and become consumed by that focus, because that lack of balance with outside interests can lead to a fall. It is vital to learn how to turn off from work, or you will become bored, run-down and unmotivated.

It is quite funny I have been accused of being complacent in 1994 because, if anything, I was too much the other way. I was focused 100 per cent on swimming in 1993 and 1994, so I had nothing else in my life.

I just swam and I didn't mix much. I trained by myself and often came home to an empty house during the day. My friends were either at work or at university. It is not surprising then I started to lose enthusiasm for swimming.

I learnt from this and my focus on swimming is now about 70 per cent and I always make sure I have outside interests, like having coffee with friends or surfing down the Gold Coast. Now when I am away from the pool I am always conscious of avoiding thinking and talking about swimming so it does not again consume my life.

Boredom

A race is not won on the day but in the months of training leading up to it. You need the right attitude for training to be effective, but this is impossible if you are bored. Boredom can harm any campaign because it stifles enjoyment and motivation.

So many people get to the block before the race and think, 'I want to win this', but they really need that aggressive and hungry attitude in training because that is where all the hard work is done.

I swam the same training program from 1992 to 1994. By 1994 I had training down pat. I lacked that hungry feeling and instead was just going through the motions. I can distinctly remember getting into the lane by myself, sticking the program at the end of the pool and just ticking off every session until I got to the end. Sometimes I could spend a whole training session without talking to anybody, including Mr Wakefield.

I never missed training once but at the same time I never really wanted to be there. I was putting in the hours but was probably only training at 80 per cent intensity. It resulted in a lack of fitness which could easily be exposed under such a heavy competition schedule as mine at the 1994 Commonwealth Games.

My problems with training made me realise I needed to make changes with my swimming to improve at the international level. In the past, Mr Wakefield's squad had a lot of swimmers my age and so I had a lot of friends and training was fun. But by the early 1990s most of the older swimmers had left and I was training by myself. I needed a stimulating squad environment where I could race against swimmers of a similar standard and interact with people my own age. This way training would no longer be boring and I could regain my enjoyment and hunger for hard work, which would benefit my race performance.

Lost confidence

Self-belief and confidence are probably the two most important ingredients in achieving the winning focus.

All the factors I've mentioned eroded my confidence over 1993 and '94 until finally my confidence was at a career low.

Everybody goes through doubts, and when the doubts start, that's when you lose confidence.

Although people comment on my quiet nature, in the pool I was known as an aggressive and confident swimmer. I lost this quality for much of those two years. Instead of producing attacking swims I became more defensive, which was especially evident at the 1994 Commonwealth Games.

When you lack confidence and self-belief you start to worry about your opposition. In 1994 I showed just how fragile my confidence was when I became concerned about other swimmers catching me in races. This was especially the case for the 100m butterfly final at the 1994 Commonwealth Games. I had remembered coach Gennadi Touretski telling me in 1993 that I would lose the 100m butterfly to my Australian team-mate Petria Thomas if I didn't change my training. At that stage my confidence was so fragile I started to believe him. That warning came back to haunt me.

I was plagued by negative thoughts, such as maybe I was never meant to win the 100m butterfly at the Commonwealth Games. I had lost the same event by less than a second at the 1990 Games. It is just amazing how powerful your mind is and how things can play on your mind if you let them. And the doubts were eating away at my confidence.

I still may have been the Australian champion and record holder but it did not give me the belief I could win the 100m butterfly. I was convinced I would not beat Petria. I stood on the blocks and I did not want to be there. So it's not surprising that I lost the race to Petria. It was frustrating to lose by just 0.03 of a second to Petria, who won in 1:00.21.

The 100m butterfly was probably the most upsetting loss because it meant I missed the medley relay, which also won a gold medal. So after that race I had really lost two gold medals.

After such a career low, the 200m butterfly became the most important race of the meet, even of my career so far. No-one but myself knew how much was riding on this race. I knew if I lost, my career would be over because I felt I could not sink any lower with my swimming. I had always felt this was *my* event, and I don't think in my vulnerable state I would have handled it well if it was also taken from me.

I had lost so much confidence it took a huge effort to get in the right focus. I realised I needed this win to regain some of my confidence and self-belief. I wanted to prove to myself I was still capable of the Olympic championship.

A lot of people have commented how white my face was when I walked out for the 200m butterfly final but if they only knew the turmoil going on inside me they would have understood. I have never felt more nervous before a race. I was determined to win this event after my earlier disappointments and I took it out from the start and won in 2:09.96, a new Commonwealth Games record. It was a relief to win and to also know I would continue to swim, because deep down I knew I wasn't ready to retire.

The win became the first brick in the foundation to rebuild my confidence. I had emerged from a big valley. The first step in the climb to a peak has to leave its impression somewhere and the 200m butterfly at the 1994 Commonwealth Games became the start of my goal to win an Olympic gold medal in 1996. The key to rebuilding my confidence was to learn to forget about my competitors and to swim my own race.

I also learnt from those Games that no matter how low your career and confidence sink, there is always a chance to start again.

CHAPTER
FOCUS

- Everyone has highs and lows but it is always possible to turn a low into a high.

- No matter how painful, don't be afraid to analyse what went wrong because often a low can lead to better understanding and improvements that start your journey to a high.

- A positive mental approach is the first step to success.

- A balanced and strong mental and physical preparation can only contribute to a successful competition.

CHAPTER TWO

SELF-DOUBT

'You all have powers you never dreamed of.
You can do things you never thought you
could do. There are no limitations in what
you can do except the limitations in your
own mind as to what you cannot do. Don't
think you cannot. Think you can.'
DARWIN P. KINGSLEY

My mouth was dry, I mean *really* dry. There was a bin next to where I was sitting and I was trying to get rid of that dry taste by spitting it out into the bin, but it didn't seem to be working. I just didn't feel right. Nothing would get rid of the nervous feeling that was overtaking me. I was so petrified I started to feel sick. I dived in and I knew I would not be able to reach the other side.

I was nine years old and was competing in a regional carnival for my school, St Agnes, at the old Valley pool in Brisbane. I had been selected in the relay and I was the second swimmer.

It was a warm Queensland summer day and the water felt refreshing as I plunged in and then surfaced. Automatically one arm came over, followed by the next arm over, as I surged closer to the halfway mark. I tried to will myself to keep going but it was no use. I had convinced myself I could not reach the other side.

I felt overwhelmed and became physically sick at the thought of putting my head in the water. My breathing started to shorten and then I seemed to forget to breathe. I felt a claustrophobic sensation, like the feeling you get in big surf when you become scared and can't breathe. Everything became surreal and seemed to crawl to slow motion. My teacher and other adults were at the side of the pool. I could hear words of encouragement to keep going but the words didn't seem to have meaning. All I could feel and think was panic.

I had to be dragged out of the pool in a humiliating exit and I was consumed by embarrassment made worse because it was a relay and my team-mates must have been upset at my non-performance. My teacher was really good, and instead of being mad she was understanding. But I'm sure everyone in the stadium that day would have doubted I would one day go on to represent Australia, let alone attempt to win an Olympic gold. I could not finish a race for my school, let alone my country.

Looking back, I don't know why I didn't give up swimming.

This wasn't a one-off situation. I barely finished one freestyle race in three years. You would think the string of humiliations would be enough to either make me stop swimming or to give me the determination to reach the other side. But nothing seemed to work. I continued to psych myself out before the races started and I couldn't finish the race whether I was coming first or I was back in the pack.

It was weird because I had no problem in training, but things changed once it got to the racing stage. I had fun at training and it became one of the few redeeming things about swimming. The other was that I enjoyed backstroke, because I didn't have to put my head in the water.

Backstroke became my saving grace. At Queensland championships I couldn't finish freestyle races and often wouldn't dare attempt a butterfly race, but backstroke was a different story. I won state and national titles in backstroke. Yet deep down I knew I couldn't rely on swimming backstroke all my life. One day I had to gain the courage to put my head in the water in races. Backstroke was only a short-term solution to achieving success.

I believe my inability to finish races could be linked to my first swimming teacher, who taught me when I was about six or seven years old. The pool policy was if you got scared and swam over to the side, they would throw you back into the middle. I remember being picked up and then swung by my arms back into the pool. I can't remember too much else but it must have been scary for somebody just coming to grips with the art of swimming. It's hard to know if this was the exact reason for the fear I experienced in races, but I don't think the situation was helped by the fact I was shy and lacked belief in myself.

When I was at primary school swimming lessons we had to put up our hand to show if we could swim 25 metres. I could swim but because I was so shy I was afraid to put up my hand. So I ended up in the group who were learning how to blow bubbles, until someone realised I could swim and they put me in the higher group.

I went to Mr Wakefield when I was nine years old and he helped me beat my early self-doubts. I found the training fun but it was with my racing Mr Wakefield really made a difference. I worked on being relaxed before my races and he gave me breathing exercises to practise. He would tell me to concentrate on my breathing before I dived in, like slow breathing in and out.

It still took ages for me to shake the habit of not finishing races and backstroke remained my best stroke from 10 to 12 years, but the focus on relaxation and on my breathing worked. I was so busy trying to breathe properly I forgot about my fears. By this time I was starting to win races and I am sure my new-found success also would have helped to erase a lot of my early self-doubts.

I still get the occasional panic attack when I'm in a hard training set or before races and whenever I do, I go back to the basic solution of relaxing and focusing on my breathing. I also try to think about something else besides swimming. It helps if you can take your mind off your race because it is easy to tense up if you think too much about what you are about to do.

So my swimming career almost didn't get going. It was a great feeling to finally conquer that crippling self-doubt. I'm glad I persevered because now I really enjoy competition, especially when I finish a race. It all comes back to your mental approach, and I learnt to believe I could reach the other side.

FACING EARLY DOUBTS: 1982–88

Often your first doubts are the hardest to conquer because when you are young you don't look at the big picture. Patience and perseverance are the best ways to conquer early doubts and hurdles because you are building your knowledge and confidence for handling future obstacles and doubts. Giving up and listening to your early doubts is a hard habit to overcome as you get older.

I was always a water baby and my first memories are of spending Christmas holidays at the Gold Coast. I started swimming lessons with Mr Wakefield in 1982, the year the Commonwealth Games came to Brisbane. The following year I wrote in a school project that one day I wanted to represent Australia in swimming, but it was a dream which came with a lot of doubts. I don't think I ever seriously saw myself as an Olympian.

I went on to taste some success at primary school swimming but I was never a child star. I didn't swim well in every event but I suppose I showed some promise. Without knowing it, this lack of success was helping to build my character because I always felt I had to work hard. And this attitude helped me in the long run because it taught me perseverance and gave me a good work ethic.

As an 11-year-old I won a state backstroke title and gained a national title the following year. Then, one year later, I went through a rough time. I was putting in the work and I registered slight improvements in my times, but I felt left behind with my swimming. My progress was far from spectacular. As a 13-year-old this was difficult to understand. I wasn't looking at the future benefits of hard work but for immediate reward for all the effort. When success didn't come instantly, I started to really doubt myself and I tried to find excuses to give up swimming. Additionally, all my friends at school seemed to be having more fun. I too wanted to just come home from school and muck around and not have to swim up and down a black line.

So every Friday afternoon Mum would say to me, 'Well, you don't have to go, you can stop swimming if you want'. She always put the decision back on me and somehow I always felt like I wanted to go. I knew deep down that I was capable of going faster and I didn't want to give up before I got to that stage. At university we learnt about inner motivation in sports psychology and I don't know if Mum realised it but that's exactly what she was using.

I'm glad I kept swimming. At the time, it was just that I had seen what other people were doing and it seemed the grass was greener on the other side. Without realising it I showed patience and perseverance, two traits that helped me to become a better swimmer. Firstly, I just kept doing the best I could to stay in touch with my age group, and second, I changed my emphasis in training. I had always focused on backstroke but now I no longer enjoyed as much success with that stroke, I started to do more butterfly and freestyle. My brother, John, swam a lot when he was young and he had a natural butterfly rhythm. Maybe that butterfly rhythm ran in the family but something inside me seemed to click with butterfly. It came naturally to me.

Furthermore, I was born severely pigeon-toed. My parents took me to several doctors and specialists but there was nothing to be done except hope I would grow out of it. Thankfully my pigeon toes never stopped me from running around and living a normal childhood but there was still some doubt about how I would cope with competitive sport. Instead of hampering my progress in the pool, however, it had the opposite effect. Having feet faced inward, my flexible ankles proved a perfect combination for butterfly.

Thirdly, I believe what also contributed to my new-found success as a 14-year-old was that I had only now started to develop. I had a growth spurt and so, physically, I was starting to catch up. The new stroke and late development combined to make the biggest improvements in my career. In that year I improved six seconds in the 100m butterfly and 12 seconds in the 200m butterfly. Now I no longer doubted I could reach the other side of the pool. But more importantly, I would not have known I had a natural talent for butterfly if I hadn't persisted. Suddenly, after such a difficult time as a 13-year-old, I began to win some butterfly races as a 14-year-old. I had overcome my early doubts and was armed with patience and perseverance for the next hurdle.

LEARNING TO ERASE SELF-DOUBTS

Everyone is confident in one or several parts of his or her life but still carries self-doubt. It is healthy to have doubt because it keeps you honest and aware of any potential pitfall. The key is not to let your doubt control you. Confidence comes when you feel comfortable and in control of the situation. Whenever you carry a self-doubt there is always a risk of failure; the more self-doubt and the risk of failure increases. So you need the confidence to carry over into all aspects of your life to experience total success, including belief in yourself and in your ability to complete the challenge you are about to undertake, whether it is an important sales meeting, to reach your goal weight or to pass your end-of-year exams.

There were several self-doubts I had to overcome early in my career. It was impossible for me to experience total success because I always carried a doubt. The main obstacle in my early career was a lack of self-belief. I listened to and believed my self-doubts so I never saw myself as a great swimmer. I eventually overcame my self-doubts to climb from an unknown schoolgirl in 1988 to the Olympic medal dais in 1992, when I won a bronze medal in Barcelona.

Dealing with disappointment

Everybody experiences disappointment in their lives but it is good to learn from an early age how to overcome and rise above it. Instead of dwelling on a disappointment and letting it develop into a doubt, use it as motivation to succeed the next time.

I was 14 years old when I competed nationally at open level for the first time, in the 1988 Olympic trials in Sydney. I felt I was at the trials for the experience and never once thought I had a chance to make the team bound for Seoul. It helped not having any real idea of what I was swimming for and not taking much notice of who I was swimming against. I loved racing open when I was young because there was no expectation; few people had heard of me. I was less nervous than I was for my age races, which would have only helped my performance.

I surprised everyone, especially myself, by finishing second in the 100m butterfly behind West Australian Fiona Allessandri. Each country is allowed two swimmers per individual event at the Olympics. Unfortunately I narrowly missed the automatic selection time so I relied on the selectors to gain an Olympic berth. The selectors may have thought I was too young and too much of a dark horse to warrant selection, so I experienced the disappointment of being very close yet still missing an Olympic team.

Mr Wakefield wrote in my yearbook for 1988 that my result should have brought Olympic selection: 'There was no doubt you were robbed and I would not have blamed you if you had retired then but to your great credit and my great relief, you continued to swim on to even greater success.'

After a big setback it is easy to start to doubt yourself, which is exactly what I did. Following that dramatic improvement between 1987 and 1988, it frustratingly took me another two years to improve in the 100m butterfly. My times stagnated. It was strange going from improving with every swim in 1988 to having a letdown. My dad always wondered whether I would have kept improving if I had gone to the Olympics because I was on an uphill curve. It would have been interesting to see how far I would have gone if I had been given the chance to compete against the world's best as a 14-year-old.

At the time I took the attitude that I was young and there were bigger things ahead but now I believe going to those Olympics would have helped me gain confidence and strength for the 1992

Olympics. Few swimmers have the experience and belief to win gold at their first Olympics so I feel the 1988 Olympics would have only benefited my Barcelona performance.

Initially I experienced doubts in my ability after missing the selection but I overcame them with the determination not to miss another opportunity. I realised I couldn't let my doubts turn into more disappointment so I persevered with hard work, which was rewarded with selection in the 1989 Australian team for the Pan Pac Championships.

It is always hard to deal with disappointment, especially when you start to doubt yourself, but it's important not to let one disappointment snowball into more disappointments. I knew I had to be mentally prepared and physically ready for my next chance of making the Australian team because I didn't want to experience disappointment and doubt again.

Finding a challenge

The best way to conquer self-doubt is to look for challenges. Once you have achieved the first challenge, you gain confidence for the next challenge. You then suddenly find yourself so busy chasing the challenges that self-doubts no longer fit in the equation.

I am naturally somebody who holds a lot of self-doubts but I found once I hopped on the escalator of challenges that I was so busy climbing to the next challenge that the self-doubts were slowly left behind. Missing the national team for the 1988 Olympics gave me the challenge of becoming an Australian representative at the 1989 Pan Pacific Championships. Despite the self-doubts I carried about myself and my swimming, I knew the only way I could make the team in 1989 was to improve. It was a challenge which I accepted with hard work. Once I made the 1989 Australian team I aimed to win an international medal, which I achieved with a silver in the 100m butterfly and gold in the 4 × 100m relay at the 1990 Commonwealth Games.

As my self-doubts faded my challenges became more bold, although I still kept them realistic. I found it too daunting if the challenge was too big, so I always kept my challenges in achievable portions. I achieved my aim of making the Australian team in five events–the 100m freestyle, 100m butterfly, 50m freestyle, 4 × 100m freestyle relay and 4 × 100m medley relay – at the 1991 World Championships in Perth. There, an important challenge was to be Australia's top butterfly swimmer, which I achieved when I finished fifth in the world 100m butterfly final. I then increased my challenge to winning a medal against the world's best swimmers at the World Championships, which was a more difficult and prestigious assignment than the 1990 Commonwealth Games. I was able to tick off the challenge when I was part of the 4 × 100m medley relay team (comprising myself, Nicole Stevensen, Karen Van Wirdum and Linley Frame) which won a silver medal. Another challenge was an Australian record, which I sealed when I won the consolation 100m freestyle final.

There is so much personal satisfaction to be gained when you set yourself a challenge, no matter the size, and you achieve it. Achieving one challenge puts you on a high and makes you want to work harder for the next level. And the next challenge then seems so much closer.

You can find a challenge in every situation, whether you have just suffered failure or tasted victory. It's okay if it takes longer than expected or you never achieve your challenge. (Every time I've failed to meet a challenge it hasn't deterred me from aiming for the next challenge.) In just reaching for your challenge it's amazing how much you improve. I've learnt the most important thing about the challenge is the striving, not the success. To strive for something is a positive momentum and your mind is in a forward motion. Self-doubts are a negative force and only propel you backwards. It is only when your challenge becomes stronger than your self-doubt that you can fly forward.

Making your environment a comfort zone

Often when you enter a new workplace or new environment it is difficult to settle in. It is natural to feel insecure and to have doubts when you are new in a position. Making a new environment a comfort zone should be one of your first priorities, because when you feel comfortable you will perform at your best.

While I was slowly becoming a poised and confident swimmer in 1988, these qualities were yet to carry over into my life out of the pool. The pool was my comfort zone and I was always glad to be back there whenever I dived in. Swimming gave me an identity and confidence, and even though I had erased some early self-doubts with my swimming I still lacked a lot of confidence in myself. So much so that the thought of competing overseas and spending several weeks with a bunch of strangers seemed scary.

Consequently, in 1988 and 1989, I half-wished I didn't make national teams because the whole experience seemed so daunting. When I was 15 years old I made the 1989 Pan Pacific team, my first Australian team, but again in some ways I didn't care if I made it or not. I found being in such a new environment more stressful than competing in the pool. My mum and I had a little cry before I left for the Pan Pac titles in Tokyo, because as well as feeling excited about representing my country there was also a lot of fear.

I swam in five events and I just cannot believe how insecure I was back then. I was glad I didn't win a medal so I wouldn't have to stand on the dais! Things didn't improve by the 1990 Commonwealth Games when I was one of several Australian representatives chosen for a special catwalk appearance at a Speedo launch, just before we left for the Games in Auckland. I was the only new member of the group chosen while most were a lot older than me, like Lisa Curry-Kenny, Angus Waddell, Andrew Baildon, Julie McDonald, Jodie Clatworthy and Glen

Housman. I found it a bit embarrassing to parade in my togs on the catwalk but the bus trip back from Sydney to Canberra was worse.

I didn't really fit in with the older athletes and on the way back from the launch we stopped off for lunch. Everyone said they would get some lunch and then eat it on the bus. So I went and got my lunch and came back to the bus. The others must have decided to stay in the restaurant and eat it there. So I was a Nigel out in the bus, eating my lunch alone, while everyone else was together in the restaurant. I felt intimidated and unconfident among a group of athletes, many of whom had been swimming for years and were such legends. I was so far away from my comfort zone.

It has been friendship which helped to dissolve the barriers and erase my doubts about where I fitted in with the team. Friendship was my key in making Australian teams and international competitions part of my comfort zone, although it was a process that took a couple of years. Since 1990 Andrew Baildon no longer has been a stranger but has become one of my best friends. I roomed with Donna Proctor at the 1989 Pan Pacs, and Donna and I hit it off straight away and have been good friends ever since. It was great to be one of the younger ones on the team because the older ones really looked after you. They had a policy of rooming old and young swimmers together. Lara Hoovield was one of my room-mates and she was very understanding and gave me lots of advice, like getting enough sleep. Sam Riley was my room-mate for the 1991 World Championships, and we have been room-mates ever since and have become pretty close friends. Suddenly my team-mates were no longer team-mates but friends.

I spent most of my teenage years in Australian swimming teams and so consequently I did a lot of growing up in that period. Sharing some key social occasions with my team-mates was another way of feeling comfortable with being an

Australian representative. I remember my first drink. A group of athletes went out after a 1988 training camp in Canberra and I had a Kahlua and milk. It was also the first time I went to a nightclub.

The 1990 Commonwealth Games was a really close team which made for a great atmosphere. I had my first big night when I pretended to be asleep in bed at nine o'clock on the last night of the Games, but instead, a group of us, including Donna, snuck out to a nearby bar. The Games finished with a team trip to Rotorua where we did some white-water rafting, went on flying foxes and rode on go-carts, which was another important team-bonding exercise.

Then, on the last night of the 1991 World Title trials in Brisbane, we all celebrated together at a local nightclub. At the 1991 World Titles I roomed with Sam Riley, Donna Proctor and Leah Broderick and we made a mobile and hung it from our ceiling. Then at the 1992 Olympics Sam Riley, Elli Overton, myself and Angus Waddell went out to try Spanish food and all the athletes finished at the nightclub Studio 54.

Every competition had a fond social memory and the memories soon linked up to form a strong comfort zone. Don't underestimate the importance of social occasions. I wasn't a rampaging party-goer but some select outings, after the hard and serious work of competition was over, helped my progress in gaining confidence. New friendships gave me new confidence out of the pool. I realised I could no longer doubt I belonged on the Australian team. I found the longer I was in Australian teams, the more comfortable I felt and the more successful I became.

Overcoming myths and hype

It is common for myths to develop at workplaces, especially around particular people. Some people have an aura about them whether it is of their own making or somebody else's. It is important not to become hooked by the hype, to be able to dig past the myths and find the truth. The playing field will never be equal while you feel your competitor possesses an aura.

I learnt one of my most important lessons at the 1990 Commonwealth Games when I came face to face with the media hype of Lisa Curry-Kenny. I had to race Lisa in Auckland. Lisa and Tracey Wickham seemed like superstars when I was nine years old during the 1982 Commonwealth Games. Then Lisa married another superstar, ironman Grant Kenny, in the late 1980s and this famous couple just seemed so daunting.

Lisa was making a comeback at the 1990 Commonwealth Games after becoming a mother a couple of years before. She received huge media coverage leading to Auckland. As a 16-year-old schoolgirl I was intimidated by the media circus surrounding her and her entourage, including Grant Kenny, who was always on pool deck. Lisa was seen as the ultimate golden girl. She was a famous swimmer and now I had to race against her. She didn't seem real but was like a myth. In my eyes she carried an aura of invincibility.

I was coached by Ken Wood at the 1990 Commonwealth Games and he gave me a lot of practical tips. He told me I was capable of beating Lisa, especially after his swimmer Karen Van Wirdum upset Lisa in the 100m freestyle the day before. But I was overpowered by the Lisa Curry-Kenny juggernaut. I fell into the trap of believing what was written in the newspapers. Lisa was portrayed in the media as this superhuman swimmer, which added to my own self-doubts. I lacked the confidence in my own ability to overcome Lisa and her aura. I was beaten on the blocks before I even started the race.

It was a very close race and I was leading after the first 50 metres by 0.13 seconds and finished less than half a second behind Lisa. She had the experience and came home strongly while I stuffed up a few little things. I was new at high-pressure international racing. In the last 25 metres I was looking at how she was going instead of concentrating on my race and my stroke. Then I missed my finish, which cost me more precious time.

Lisa had 1991 off and then made a highly publicised comeback in 1992. But this time I was ready and was not over-awed. I had learnt from my experience in Auckland and I wasn't going to make the same mistake again. After 1990 I realised how close I came to a gold medal when before I doubted I would ever get near a medal. Winning a silver medal gave me the confidence to know I was well and truly in the chase for success. I knew I could turn it around the next time I raced Lisa. I had given Lisa a mental advantage in 1990 but now I knew I was racing just Lisa and not the aura I had created around her. We were on the same footing and suddenly I found the belief I could win. I was able to overcome my doubts and Lisa never beat me again.

Lisa and I are different personalities and while she was someone who was comfortable in the limelight, I tended to shy away from it. One particular occasion I remember was the 1992 Queensland Titles and Lisa received a lot of publicity as part of her comeback bid to make the Barcelona Olympics. When she walked confidently in front of me in her colourful bikinis and flexed her abdominal muscles in the warm-up for the 50m freestyle, I was no longer the rookie schoolgirl intimidated by her. I no longer saw her as a myth but as an equal. I knew then I had the confidence to beat her.

She was the favourite and I had already swum and won the 200m freestyle a couple of races before the 50m freestyle so I was not expected to figure in the calculations. But I made sure I had plenty in reserve to not only upset her but swim a personal best in the 50m freestyle.

I suppose it was my way of proving to myself how far I had progressed since the 1990 Commonwealth Games. It was a personal milestone. In Auckland I had let myself down by caving in to my doubts and the hype surrounding a rival. I had made it tough for myself because it is just about impossible to beat somebody who is veiled in the aura of invincibility. It took a major career loss in 1990 for me to see through the myths and erase my self-doubts. Since then I try never to stand in the shadow of awe.

Handling your first success

We spend our lives chasing success but not many of us are taught how to handle it. We learn how to chase challenges but not how to deal with the situation when we achieve them. Like everything with a novice, there are traps and downfalls to be aware of so that your first success does not become your last.

My first major success was at the 1991 Pan Pacific Championships in Canada when I not only won my first international individual gold medal but achieved it in an amazing fashion. I became the first swimmer in the Commonwealth to break the elusive one minute barrier in the 100m butterfly when I swam a 59.93 second race. I defeated a world class field, finishing ahead of Xiaohong Wang of China and Chrissy Ahmann-Leighton of the United States. Suddenly the challenges had stacked up and I was at a level I had not expected to reach. I had achieved major international success and to say I was on a huge high was an understatement.

It was my first international success and it did wonders in helping me shake off my self-doubts. After the 1991 Pan Pacs I realised I could match it with international swimmers. It became a turning point in how I thought about myself in relation to the world. Before then I had been plagued by doubts that I was not as good as the Americans and Europeans. In my eyes the Americans seemed to be world champions in everything they did and just about impossible to beat. They were always so sure of themselves and usually the loudest on pool deck.

Ken Woods, who was my coach at the 1991 Pan Pacific Titles, played a big part in helping me gain the self-belief I could beat swimmers from other countries. He told me it didn't matter what I had done in the past but it only counted what I was going to do in the next two laps. He made me realise the only thing that mattered was what took place in the race. A famous saying of his was 'When the flag drops, the bullshit stops'. After learning to surmount new challenges I finally possessed the crucial self-belief to conquer my next challenge when I dived in for the 100m butterfly final. I had overcome my self-doubts and beaten a world class field. It was the first time in my career an Olympic gold medal did not seem so elusive. Suddenly being the best in the world seemed an achievable challenge.

Success is often a turning point. But not many people realise that success is high maintenance. Some people taste success but don't have the stomach for the extra work while others feed from it. I was determined not to fall into the trap of thinking I had achieved everything and I didn't need to work as hard.

Instead of seeing it as a sign to scale down my work, I knew I needed to work even harder. I remember coming back from Canada and starting to train straight away. My intensity in training increased and I was the most committed I had ever been with my swimming.

Once you experience success you realise how close you are to more success. Instead of being full on success, I was even more hungry. I learnt success should keep you hungry and excited for more success. This attitude helped me with my training leading to the 1992 Olympic Games. I was determined to taste success again.

A calculated risk

You know when you have overcome self-doubt, when you have the courage to make a calculated risk. It is easy to continue on the same path, especially when you have experienced success. Most successes come from a risk but without self-belief it is impossible to take that risk. By looking at the big picture, analysing your best opportunity, and conquering your self-doubts, a well-planned risk often pays off.

I am not a risk-taker by nature so when Mr Wakefield suggested after the 1991 Pan Pacific Titles to concentrate on the 200m butterfly event (an event I had never seriously raced in competition) instead of the 100m butterfly, I was flabbergasted. After my first major international success in what I believed was my main event, the 100m butterfly, it took several weeks for Mr Wakefield to convince me. It seemed to me it was a natural progression to race the 100m butterfly at the 1992 Olympics after beating several of my main Barcelona rivals at the 1991 Pan Pacific Titles. One of the reasons I queried the 200m butterfly was it required more work. I had to put in more kilometres to increase my stamina. But I put in the hard work to give the risk the best chance of coming off. I started to train for the 200m butterfly only about six months away from the Olympics.

I turned up to the 1992 Queensland Titles to compete in the 200m butterfly and the marshalling lady just laughed at me, she thought it was the biggest joke. I was seen as a sprinter and not as a distance swimmer. Amazingly, I clicked with the 200m butterfly straight away. I won the Queensland Championships but I still came into the Olympic trials as the underdog. Hayley Lewis was the reigning Commonwealth champion and Julie Majer and Helen Morris were also favourites.

Incredibly, after just limited racing experience in the event, I not only won the trial but I broke the Commonwealth record. By the time I competed in Barcelona I had raced the 200m butterfly just six times yet I managed to win a bronze medal. I had improved by five seconds in only six months and who knew what I was capable of with more training behind me. In Barcelona I still competed in the 100m butterfly. Mr Wakefield's calculated risk proved correct because I finished fifth, which obviously was not the same as a bronze medal.

Mr Wakefield based the risk on the fact that the 200m butterfly was a more open event nationally and internationally than the 100m butterfly. He saw it as my best chance to win an Olympic medal. Mr Wakefield always said I had a good aerobic capacity so he must have seen I had a natural leaning for stamina work. Maybe he thought the 200m butterfly was an ideal event for me because it required stamina but also some speed to sprint home. Whatever his thoughts, Mr Wakefield knew what he was doing. In just six months I had found my niche in swimming, as a 200m butterfly specialist. Without taking that risk I never would have experienced my success. And by my taking that calculated risk with him it proved I was no longer shackled by heavy self-doubts. It just showed how much confidence I could have to achieve in an event I was just a novice at.

An Olympic bronze medal in 1992 was a dream come true but I knew I would not have scaled such a height if I was still weighed down by the self-doubts I had when I first started to swim. It is human to doubt and self-doubts keep you honest, but the trick is not to let your life become over-run by doubts. After 1992 I realised I was still not in complete control of all my self-doubts, otherwise I would have won the gold medal. I knew I needed total self-belief to win Olympic gold in 1996 and this became my mission in the four years leading to Atlanta: to be master of my self-doubts.

CHAPTER
FOCUS

- Giving up and listening to your doubts becomes a hard habit to break. Patience and perseverance will overcome any obstacle or doubt.

- Don't let disappointment snowball into doubt and more disappointment.

- The best way to conquer self-doubt is to strive towards a challenge. You can go forward only if the positive momentum of your challenge overpowers the negative force of self-doubt.

- You can achieve a maximum performance only if you are comfortable in your environment.

- Never stand in the shadow of awe but see through the hype so that you are competing only against your rival and not the aura surrounding him or her.

- Success should not leave you full but hungry for more success.

- Never be afraid to take a calculated risk.

CHAPTER THREE

FAIR PLAY

'You have a choice in life . . . choose to win.'

'The only limits on human achievement are self-imposed.'

DR DENNIS WAITLEY

It is not surprising that Laurie Lawrence, the most colourful character in Australian swimming, dreamt up one of the best descriptions of the muscle-bound Chinese swimmers. He remembered 200m individual medley gold medallist Li Lin as a little girl at the 1988 Olympics but just four years later, in Barcelona, Lawrence said she was unrecognisable with a back 'like Tasmania's best axe-man'.

I have a picture in my scrapbook of butterfly rival Xiaohong Wang emerging from the pool at the 1992 Olympics and that description would also be fitting for her. Her shoulders and back seemed too enormous to be natural. If anything, by the 1994 World Championships in Rome, in September, the Chinese had grown in stature and they physically overshadowed their rivals.

I was fortunate I didn't have to contend with the Chinese while I was going through so much personal pain at the 1994 Commonwealth Games in Canada two weeks earlier. But the Chinese, who seemed to be powered by artificial fuel, were out in force at Rome. By the last day of the championships, only three women had stood up to the Chinese domination: German teenage superstar Franzisca van Almsick, American distance legend Janet Evans and Australian breaststroker Sam Riley were the only women to break the Chinese stranglehold.

Now it was my turn in the 200m butterfly. And I had several things in my favour. As Queensland born and bred I have always found there is nothing like it when you feel the sunshine spreading its rays on your arms and back as you lap an outdoor pool, and I experienced that sensation in Rome. I knew as soon as I saw the outdoors pool in Rome, basking in the sun, and the spectator seating, reaching for the sky, that I would love that place. I class it as one of my favourite pools, because it reminded me so much of Brisbane. When we competed it was 30 degree-plus weather and so humid, just like a sweltering Brisbane summer, and that is when I like to swim. I swim my best when I'm sweating, when I'm really hungering for that cool sensation of diving into the water. The afternoon sun was beating down strongly while we waited in marshalling for the final.

And it wasn't just the sun but also the overwhelming support of the crowd when we walked to our positions behind the starting blocks. I had finished third in the 100m butterfly behind Limin Liu and Yun Qu earlier in the meet. I suppose people saw me as the only chance at stopping yet another Chinese victory. I had been given a boost by clocking my fastest heat swim since the 1992 Barcelona Olympics, which had remained the setting for my personal best.

In the slow walk from the marshalling area to the starting blocks the support was amazing. Countries were grouped together in the stands and as I passed each country, other swimmers would yell, 'Come on, Susie. You can beat them for us.' *Us* was me and thousands of others in the stands and in the worldwide television audience. *Them* was the Chinese. The more successful the Chinese became, the more vocal the crowd became in support of their rivals.

The message from the crowd was pretty clear. Hardly anyone cheered when the Chinese won. The Chinese would stand on the medal dais and go 'Yeah' and hold their hands up in triumph and everyone would just sit still in the stands. The silence was deafening. But probably the clearest message came from a placard a spectator carried. He had a metre-long cardboard cut-out of a needle and as the Chinese athletes walked passed, he would push the fake needle into his arm. But the Chinese seemed oblivious of the crowd and their potent messages. They always just smiled and waved.

The sunshine and the support of such a huge crowd should have given me the strength I needed for victory. But it was too late. The damage had already been done. By the last day I had become brainwashed that the huge Chinese women were unbeatable.

The Chinese had won almost every women's event and everyone was talking about how they were on drugs and the talk seemed to increase their unbeatable status. Again, with my confidence low, I fell into the trap of listening to others instead of drawing on my inner strength and self-belief.

It was easy to believe the talk once you saw the size of most of the Chinese swimmers. Chinese sprint queen Le Jingyi's back was enough to scare anybody. She became the symbol of the Chinese women's sudden domination and hence had the most photographed back in the world. The rippling muscles made many of the male swimmers envious of her size. But besides her massive shoulders she was pretty skinny and had a relatively small waist and hips. She was so out of proportion. She wasn't just a show-stopper out of the pool either. She broke four world records in the 50m and 100m freestyle and in two relays and was named swimmer of the championships.

In my training leading to the World Championships I'd already acknowledged I couldn't beat the Chinese in sprints. Their domination of the 50m and 100m events had prompted me to concentrate on the 200m butterfly and 200m freestyle. Their times were superhuman and there was just no point in my putting so much effort into freestyle sprint training when I was nowhere near the same range. It is always important to be aware of your capabilities and know where to direct your energy. I knew I was never going to be a 53 and 54 second swimmer for the 100m freestyle. I knew I would never beat Le Jingyi over that distance. This may seem a negative attitude but the Chinese sprint domination probably helped me with my heavy schedule. It meant I could focus on preparing for the 200m butterfly.

At the World Championships Sam Riley beat the Chinese but I couldn't muster the confidence that I could do the same in my pet event, the 200m butterfly. There was no doubt Sam's Chinese rivals were on drugs. Sam's coach Scott Volkers told me how one of the Chinese swimmers acted very suspiciously after the race. She had tried to run away from the drug testers and was chased around the pool. She then tried to escape by jumping over a hedge before being finally caught.

It was exciting to watch Sam not only beat the Chinese, who were twice her size, but also break the 100m breaststroke world record. In 1994 I didn't have the mental strength or confidence to save the world from the Chinese.

Standing on the blocks, I was already beaten. In my mind China had already won their twelfth gold medal of the meet. I had set myself my limit before the race had started – I had chosen to lose.

I was hemmed in between Limin and Yun in the final. I was surrounded by acne-scarred faces, deep voices and Adam's apples, although Limin was probably one of the more feminine-looking Chinese swimmers. She was one of the few who didn't have facial hair and a deep voice.

I aimed for and expected the bronze medal. After such a terrible Commonwealth Games I accepted it without a fight. I was even happy with two bronze medals behind the Chinese. My confidence had taken such a battering in 1993 and 1994 that by the World Championships I couldn't raise my customary fire. I was usually a fierce competitor in the pool but that hunger to win was missing. And the rampaging Chinese threw the final blow to my shattered confidence.

I was still in the race with one lap to go but then the Chinese took off and I gave up. Now I will never know how I would have gone given the right attitude and focus. I acknowledged defeat too easily. Every race should be contested, no matter what advantages the other competitors seem to have. I was the only swimmer at the World Championships to win a bronze medal twice behind two Chinese, Limin and Yun. I wish now that I'd been more vocal about the Chinese and the drug rumours but I was conscious of being seen as a bad loser when there was no proof the Chinese I raced were on drugs.

While I missed out on two gold medals, the media did give me one title – Australia's unluckiest swimmer.

SUSPICIONS: 1989–94

'Racing the Chinese girls who have faces like Mack trucks.' I was preparing to race the 100m butterfly and this was my line in Laurie Lawrence's daily inspirational poems for the 1992 Olympics. He was referring to the massive size and often masculine features of the Chinese female swimmers at Barcelona that I had to race, including Hong Quian, who ended up winning the 100m butterfly. It was at these Olympics that the suspicions about China and drug use really became a hot issue.

I first raced the Chinese in 1989 in China on my international debut, and at that time none of the Chinese swimmers stood out with a muscle-bound body or as being exceptionally fast. China were not a huge force in 1989 but were on the rise. No Chinese swimmer made the final in the 1984 Olympics, but by 1988 there were 10 finalists. In 1988 the East German women were the major force following Kristin Otto's six-gold medal haul. There were rumours when we were in China and in the years following that East German scientists had set up base in China. In 1989 I would never have imagined the Chinese becoming my biggest threat.

Canadian coach Dave Johnson was the first outspoken critic of China's sudden rise in women's swimming when he issued a warning at the 1991 World Championships. The Chinese achieved a quinella in the 100m butterfly with Hong Quian and Xiaohong Wang and finished behind the United States as top nation with eight gold medals, three silver and two bronze. But surprisingly, China's sudden improvement was not treated as a big thing. And, importantly, leading to Barcelona there was no out-of-competition drug testing to keep swimmers honest.

Dave Johnson's warnings became reality at the 1992 Olympics. Suddenly, in Barcelona, where it mattered, the Chinese had become a dominant unit. China achieved 13 finalists and four gold medals, two of them in world record time. Xiaohong Wang just touched me out for a silver medal in the 200m butterfly at Barcelona and was one of five Chinese silver medallists. What gave ammunition to critics is that only one of the medals came in an event that was over 200m and no Chinese men made a final.

There was a lot of feeling among the swimmers and coaches that the Chinese were cheating a generation of swimmers out of their dues. When Laurie Lawrence congratulated one of the Chinese coaches he was angrily asked by an American coach why he would congratulate 'cheating bastards'. At the same time the world swimming body, FINA, seemed to be taking the soft approach. FINA's drug-testing policy was to test randomly only two of the top four finishers. So 100m freestyle champion Zuang Yong, with her deep voice, heavy muscles and bad acne, escaped the drug test.

The rumours and suspicions were well in force by the end of Barcelona. There were stories about China's Minister for Sport being forced to resign after 1988 because China didn't win enough medals, but his successor obviously didn't have the same problem in 1992. There was a rumour about big laboratories being set up near pools in China so scientists could work closely with the swimmers.

I don't remember the Chinese doubling in size from one meet to another so I think it was a gradual process. By 1993 most of the Chinese had deep voices, acne, Adam's apples and brown teeth. My main memory of 1993 is hearing the deep voices of the Chinese in the change rooms. The joke was whenever you heard a deep voice you would wrap your towel around you, just in case it was a man, but it was one of the Chinese female swimmers. There were always rumours circulating about the Chinese. One of the more exotic was how the Chinese would rip off turtle heads and then drink the blood – that was their secret tonic.

To add fuel to the fire the Chinese had pulled out of the 1993

Pan Pacs to concentrate on their national championships. The widespread belief in the Australian camp was China pulled out to avoid any steroid scandal on the eve of the September 1993 vote for the 2000 Games. Beijing was the main competitor to Sydney. Then at the Chinese national championships in early September, seven Chinese women smashed the minute barrier for the 100m butterfly in one race–a barrier only three swimmers, including myself, had broken between the Barcelona Olympics and 1993. These amazing feats probably hurt China's reputation more than anything else. Their times and achievements seemed to be too incredible to believe.

The Chinese were always ready with a reason for their rise in swimming, saying how they were the world's biggest country with a population of more than 1.3 billion to choose swimmers from, or that the secret behind their success was they trained six hours a day plus two hours in the gym. Steroids are known to aid recovery from draining daily schedules but the Chinese always maintained they were fuelled by special Chinese herbs and chicken broth, not drugs.

The 1993 World Short Course Championships stand out as the first meet that the Chinese excessively dominated. They broke 11 world records and won just about every event. I won the 100m butterfly to stop the Chinese avalanche. There was a scandal when Australian head coach Don Talbot claimed another Chinese swimmer masqueraded for the new 100m freestyle record-breaker Le Jingyi at drug testing, but obviously this was difficult to prove. There was a call for identity photographs for the next competition to avoid another suspected case of swapping names.

The International Olympic Committee and FINA turned a blind eye, which was frustrating. It seemed they didn't want to do anything when it was common knowledge the Chinese were on drugs. I suppose they didn't want to take the tough stand because it could make the sport look bad. If everyone got caught for drugs the sport could look like a joke.

Things didn't change in 1994 with Australian swimming officials exasperated when Chinese 50m and 100m butterfly world short course record-holder Zhong Weiye tested positive in a Beijing meeting but was given only a two-year suspension. Then apparently another three Chinese athletes had tested positive on the eve of the 1994 World Titles.

By the 1994 World Championships, swimming officials, coaches and swimmers were in an outspoken uproar about the Chinese. The private sniggers behind the Chinese backs were now starting to turn into a universal public protest, especially after Le Jingyi took 0.47 seconds off the 100m freestyle, the biggest chunk carved off the event since East German Kornelia Ender in 1973. By the end of the championships, 18 nations had signed a declaration calling on FINA to give drug testing a significantly higher priority.

MY RESULTS AND THE CHINESE

1991 World Championships: Fifth behind two Chinese in the 100m butterfly.

1992 Olympic Games: Third behind a Chinese in the 200m butterfly; fifth behind two Chinese in the 100m butterfly.

1993 World Short Course Championships: Second behind a Chinese in the 200m butterfly; second behind the Chinese in the 4 × 200m freestyle relay.

1994 World Championships: Third behind two Chinese in the 100m butterfly; third behind two Chinese in the 200m butterfly; fourth behind the Chinese in the 4 × 100m medley relay; fourth behind the Chinese in the 4 × 100m freestyle relay; fifth behind two Chinese in the 200m freestyle.

My Focus

I have been one of the Australian swimmers most affected by the Chinese onslaught. There are question marks over ten events in the World Championships and Olympic Games alone between 1991 and 1994, the meets in which I could have moved into the medals or changed my medal colour if the Chinese had not competed.

It is impossible to measure the implications on my career, my self-esteem and how dramatically my résumé would have changed if the Chinese were drug-free. I have never added up the damage bill until now because I have tried not to dwell too much on the past. There is a danger if you detail and focus on all the negatives that you will get down about it. On reflection, I realise how difficult it was to keep going when the situation seemed so unfair, but I never saw giving up as an option, especially when I was on a constant upward curve myself.

When the Chinese first emerged in 1991 and started to swim incredible times and win stacks of medals, I was 16 years old and a bit naive. I didn't see the wider and future implications. But I soon took notice because the Chinese dominated my events, the 100m and 200m freestyle and 100m and 200m butterfly.

When the allegations about the Chinese erupted at the 1992 Olympics we were asked to be diplomatic in media interviews by Australian Swimming management, to be careful about what we said. It was frustrating that we couldn't speak our minds but no one wanted a big public brawl. At the time I wasn't too upset because an American, Summer Sanders, won the 200m butterfly, so I didn't feel the Chinese had robbed me of a golden opportunity. Now I realise this was just the start of the Chinese domination.

I thought there was nothing I could do about the Chinese domination except ignore the talk and set my mind on beating them. It was easy to take this attitude and try not to worry about the long-term implications on my career. I heard many rumours about the Chinese but I tried not to think about it too much or ask more questions. I tried to look on the bright side and give them the benefit of the doubt.

My policy to ignore them worked in the 1993 World Short-course Titles. I remained apart from China's domination and retained my self-focus, which helped me to win. Despite my form slide, I had some self-belief that I could win. It was a confidence boost to win the 100m butterfly because it's a power event, ideal for the muscle-bound Chinese. Beating them gave me a big lift.

But in the long run ignoring them didn't work to my benefit. Some things can become too big to ignore and you are left unprepared in dealing with them. I'd never thought about my tactics against the Chinese too much, except just wanting to beat them, so when we reached the 1994 World Championships I didn't know how to deal with China's phenomenal success.

Because I didn't have my own way of approaching China's golden results, I just followed the general feeling of other swimmers and I started to worry. Before the World Championships I had acknowledged I couldn't beat the Chinese in my minor event, the 100m freestyle, so I'd focused my training on my other events, especially the 200m butterfly. I knew the longer the distance, the less assistance drugs gave. But by the time I stood on the blocks at the championships for the 200m butterfly I had no self-belief I could win. I was doing everything an elite athlete shouldn't. I was reacting to the rumours swelling around me. My approach to ignore them hadn't worked.

I remember feeling angry about the Chinese reaction to the drug-taking rumours. The Chinese brought in the racist angle by saying Western athletes were just jealous of their success. But what made me extremely angry was the lack of action by the FINA officials. It wasn't their lives that were being hurt but the athletes'. And it was especially annoying because it gave the wrong message about cheating. Athletes shouldn't feel they have to take steroids just to be in the competition, which is what happens when the use of drugs is widespread. I've never been offered drugs and fortunately I've never seen drug-taking in Australian swimming. It is just about impossible for an Australian swimmer to be on performance-enhancing drugs, because the testing is so stringent.

It annoys me when people take drugs because when you look at it, it's only a swimming event. It is unbelievable how people would jeopardise their health and wreck other people's careers for one moment of glory. Even if steroids were legal, there's no way I'd ever take steroids because of their effects. Nothing is worth harming your health.

For years the East Germans had stolen a lot of swimmers' golden moments and now it seemed it was the turn of the Chinese. After hearing how so many athletes suffered from injustice during the East German reign (1976 to 1988), suddenly it seemed I may have been at the wrong end of that same injustice. I didn't know how to feel after finishing third twice behind two Chinese. If my Chinese rivals were on drugs then it was a great achievement to be the next best in the world.

But then again I was angry because it all seemed to point to the fact I had been robbed. I wasn't too sure how outspoken I could be. It looked like I had been robbed but it was impossible to measure by how much. There is a lot of difference between winning two bronze and two gold medals at the World Championships. It seemed all I had gained were lost opportunities and there was not much I could do about it. I felt so powerless because the situation felt wrong but the official records said it was right. All I had was my right to speak out publicly, but it was hard because the Chinese had tested clean.

After the 1994 World Championships it would have been easy to be totally disillusioned but I still wanted to beat the Chinese and I thought I had a chance if I could get my preparation and focus right. In Rome I was two seconds slower than the Chinese, which I didn't feel was a big margin to overcome. I felt it was certainly a margin within my reach.

FIGHTING BACK: 1994

The 1994 World Championships in Rome was the turning point. Never before had any country dominated a meet except for the East Germans in the 1986 World Championships in Madrid, Spain, when the East German women won 13 of 16 events and the East German men won just one gold. In 1994 the Chinese women won 12 gold medals and not one Chinese male swimmer made the final. If they hadn't won so many events it wouldn't have sparked the same level of outrage. The international swimming community realised something had to be done quickly.

I believe people reacted so quickly and so publicly against the Chinese because they had seen it all before with the East Germans and no one wanted to see something like that happen again. After the World Championships the influential American-based *Swimming World* magazine refused to acknowledge the Chinese in their awards but instead Sam Riley was recognised as the world's best female swimmer in 1994. Magazine editor Dr Phil Written was quoted as saying about the drug issue: 'We've seen the movie before, we know how it ends.'

The united approach strengthened the anti-drug campaign and FINA took action. All 169 drug samples taken at the World Championships were negative. This didn't mean much because no East German tested positive in competition in the 1970s and 1980s but they were later proved to be on steroids in training. It is virtually impossible to find a positive sample at a meet because competitors expect to be tested. The key is to catch them by surprise. And this is what FINA did.

FINA made unscheduled drug-testing calls on about 17 Chinese swimmers just three days before the 1994 Asian Games in October and then more swimmers on the last day of the Games. They were clearly caught out. Not surprisingly, the Chinese had won all 15 women's swimming titles at the Asian Games. Some big fish were caught. World 400m freestyle champion Yang Aihua was exposed as one of four Chinese female swimmers who tested positive from the first lot of testing. A normal male testosterone level has a ratio of 1–1, but Yan had between 15–1 and 9–1. She was suspended for two years and became the fifth Chinese female swimmer to test positive to drugs in the two-year period until 1994.

Then it was reported 11 Chinese athletes, including eight swimmers, tested positive to the steroid dehydroxytestosterone at the Asian Games. Altogether 11 swimmers were stripped of their competition medals, although they never had their World Championships medals taken away, which is what most of the Australian swimmers wanted. The second big name caught, Lu Bin, was someone I had actually raced. She had won the 200m individual medley world title, achieved silver medals in the 100m and 200m freestyle and anchored two successful relays in Rome. Xiong Guoming, another member of China's conquering World Championships team, also tested positive. Lu and Xiong had both won four gold medals at the Asian Games and Lu even broke the 200m individual medley world record.

Japanese doctor Yoshio Kuroda, who was part of the drug-testing team, was reported saying that he suspected more of the swimmers tested were on drugs because their samples were in the grey area. They had more testosterone than the average person but it was still at the level where it could have been naturally produced. The Chinese government was reported as saying they would set up a special panel to launch an investigation and impose 'severe punishment'.

It was great so many Chinese swimmers were caught because it proved people's suspicions. FINA needed to clean it up before the next Olympics, where it really mattered. Fortunately FINA swooped and collected evidence.

After the mass of positive tests in 1994, swimmers spoke out about the Chinese, including myself. It was a relief to know they had finally been caught, that there was concrete evidence. It was becoming more and more obvious there was a systematic drug program in China. But I was still worried that the butterfly swimmers I raced against at the World Championships had not been caught, so I didn't know if my rivals were cheats.

In the summer of 1994–95 a petition to turn the two-year drug ban for positive tests to four years or life was circulated at state championships around Australia. It was supported by swimmers who were not affected in competition, such as Kieren Perkins. Kieren and the Australian Swimming Coaches Association were among those who called for all Chinese swimmers to be suspended from all competition for four years. So, by the end of 1994, FINA was responding to the injustice and the powerful groundswell of anger against drug cheats, and my fortunes were looking up against the Chinese.

Answers to the tough questions

1. How long should athletes be banned for taking performance-enhancing drugs?

I believe they should be banned for life. In 1994 officials were pushing for a four-year competition ban, but when you look at it, four years means nothing. A two-year ban is even worse because it means anyone caught could still go to the next Olympic Games. Two years out of competition is no career-threatening barrier.

You also have to look at the question of how long does the effect of a drug remain in your body. There is a line of thought that a drug and its advantages could remain in an athlete's system for several years. In which case, steroids might still help athletes a year or two after last taking them. There was a rumour a European swimming star was on steroids when she was part of the East German system. If the rumour were true, the drugs might have helped her gain her muscular physique.

The Americans were very strong anti-drug campaigners, including swimmer Angelina Martino who tested positive to steroids in 1988. She said the pill had given her a false reading. She has a deep voice and is extremely muscular but again, that is not evidence. Angelina went on to win gold and bronze medals in the 1992 and 1996 Olympics. The positive test had no effect on her achieving the ultimate in sport, an Olympic gold. She may as well not have been banned.

The only consolation in a four-year ban is the guilty swimmer is cut out of the next Olympics. To really threaten and punish cheats, it would be safer to install a life-time ban.

2. How do you catch drug cheats?

There is no doubt the science of cheating is always going to be better than the science of catching them. That is why the shame factor becomes the main weapon. It's impossible to catch every drug cheat, although candid, out-of-competition testing has helped, so really the only way to stop swimmers taking drugs is to play on their conscience and reputation. They need to know it means nothing to win a gold medal falsely.

You often hear news reports now about East German and Russian athletes who have had deformed babies, countless miscarriages and strokes as a result of using steroids. It is interesting how many of them now say their gold medals are meaningless after winning by artificial means and paying the price with their health.

There was a story in *World Swimming* magazine that reported on secret East German police files which showed Kristin Otto had more testosterone in her system than the entire starting team of the Dallas Cowboys. If the story is true, no wonder Kristin won six gold medals at the 1988 Olympics. But you have to wonder what will be the cost to her health and self-esteem in the long run, knowing she had to resort to such a significant level of artificial means to win.

Besides technology, tougher sentences for a positive result would be the answer, but a four-year ban is not an overly threatening punishment. So the only way to make athletes stop taking drugs is with the moral issue. This was the policy used against the Chinese and it worked at the 1996 Olympics. The Chinese were shamed and shunned. Instead of China being seen as a leading sporting nation, they were seen as a country of cheats.

3. Who is responsible?

It is hard to know whether the Chinese swimmers were aware they were being doped. There are conflicting reports whether government agencies, coaches, doctors or the swimmers were behind the drug use. China is a different culture from ours and maybe the swimmers saw sporting success as a chance to escape poverty. There were a lot of incentives if you swam better, like a new car, a new house or your parents were given better jobs.

Obviously it's not the swimmers' fault if they didn't know they were being doped. Everyone deserves a choice of whether they want to take drugs or not. It is the athletes who are risking their health, not the officials. Dr Yoshio Kuroda reportedly raised doubts whether 15-year-old swimmers would be capable of using the complicated and technical procedure involved with steroid use.

There is no proof every Chinese swimmer was drug-assisted. But with so many swimmers achieving extraordinary results, China's drug taking was seen as institutionalised. It is hard to know whether the rumour was true that the Chinese government sacked their Minister for Sport after the 1988 Olympics because the results weren't good enough. It is also impossible to know how far the Chinese were prepared to go to become a sport superpower. Maybe the blame for the Chinese drug disgrace of the 1990s should also be shouldered by international swimming officials who let drug cheats avoid punishment for so long.

Since the 1994 Asian Games crisis, the Chinese government has distanced itself from the scene of the crime and wants to be seen as acting tough. The government launched its own investigation into how so many Chinese swimmers tested positive and then, in September 1995, the Chinese parliament passed a law which made it an offence to supply banned drugs to athletes. The Chinese wanted to be seen to be doing the right thing and Australia was invited to help set up drug-testing facilities in China, but obviously it's hard to measure this operation's success.

Knowing who was responsible will remain a question we will never have an answer to.

HOW TO BEAT AN UNFAIR ADVANTAGE

After the 1994 World Championships I realised my focus was wrong and I wanted to be ready for any future drug cheats. China was not and will never be the only country with a drug problem. There are many individuals, from a variety of nations, who have a drug history. By the end of 1994 the worst seemed to be behind me with the Chinese caught out and shamed, but I knew I had to be prepared, especially if I decided to continue swimming to the 1996 Olympics and beyond. I realised I needed to improve my mental and physical approach to gain the extra confidence for any new threat.

Mental attitude

Coach Scott Volkers has a saying, 'Never give a sucker an even break', but unfortunately this is what I did at the 1994 World Championships when I aimed for the bronze medal. I not only gave them victory but the mental advantage. I realise now that no matter what the circumstances, you can't let your opponents break you even before the race has begun. Whether the Chinese had the advantage of drug assistance or not, I was giving them a double chance with my could-not-win attitude. No opposition deserves two advantages.

I saw the right approach for tackling the Chinese in my room-mate Sam and her coach Scott. Sam's quiet confidence never wavered and you knew her calm self-belief on the block was going to take her to victory. She was a picture of mental strength and her victories, when everyone else was folding to the Chinese domination, became an inspiration. She never gave the Chinese the advantage of believing they were invincible. Sam showed us they could be beaten.

One approach Scott used to hold the right mental attitude was by looking at the Chinese swimmers' weaknesses. He believed drugs didn't give swimmers every advantage and that the Chinese may have been powerful but it was the power-to-body-weight ratio which was the true measure. Scott figured Sam's small frame hid deceptive strength and despite the massive size of the Chinese, she held a power-to-weight advantage. He believed the right stroke and fitness would win races and not just crude strength, and this helped Sam to gain mental strength.

Winning is all about attitude. The Chinese were not unbeatable just because they used steroids. In everything you tackle you have to assess your and the opposition's strengths and weaknesses. Everybody has a weakness and by carrying the right mental attitude you can exploit it. In 1994 I found China's unbeatable tag too powerful to overcome. Now I know they've got weaknesses. They only seemed impossible to beat because I had the wrong mental attitude.

Cover all bases

The only way you can master your toughest challenge is by covering all bases. In 1994 I not only lacked confidence with my swimming but also with my preparation. I knew I could be fitter and I knew I had not done everything possible to be the best swimmer I could be. Nothing more can give you confidence than standing on the blocks before a race knowing you could not have done more to prepare for the race. With the Chinese on fire in 1994 I knew I didn't have the preparation to tackle them so I couldn't feel confident.

My preparation for 1994 was probably the worst ever because I lacked motivation. I was bored with swimming and I was burnt out. Every time the Chinese beat me I knew there was more I could have done in training. But the 1994 World Championships served as a wake-up call. Instead of feeling down about the Chinese wins, I saw the championships only really offered challenges. I knew I hadn't reached my potential and there were improvements I could make which would give me the confidence to beat my toughest competitors. It became a challenge whether backed by the right base I could bridge the two-second gap between myself and the Chinese. If I had won two gold medals at the World Championships I would not have changed my preparation. I needed such a bad 1994 Commonwealth Games and World Championships to realise I could be a better swimmer. I was hungry and desperate for gold. I couldn't help but think, Imagine what I could have achieved with the right preparation.

With the right base you can carry the power of knowing that the opposition has to do something really special to beat you. You *know* when you have gained that confidence, and you can only really carry such supreme confidence when you know you have done everything possible to achieve success.

Beating cheats

There is nothing more satisfying in achieving victory when your competitor has had more advantages. There is nothing better than beating someone who people say is unbeatable. It would have been easy to think the Chinese were just too good and to give up after the 1994 World Championships. I realised if I kept thinking the Chinese were unbeatable, then I should retire. But I became more determined, not disheartened. It gave me a lift to think with improved preparation and mental attitude, I could beat any rival. It was an inspirational thought to carry into training, knowing nothing could give me more pleasure than winning when the playing field may not be even.

It is the best feeling to know you have reached the ultimate with your own sweat and hard toil. You have gained success with your own hands and didn't need to stoop down to the level of needing artificial assistance. By taking drugs you are acknowledging you are a failure because you cannot achieve on your own merit. I knew nothing would be more satisfying than to beat those who had gone to such lengths to cheat, and it became a challenge which inspired me for the 1996 Olympics.

CHAPTER
FOCUS

- When the situation seems unfair or overwhelming, assess your capabilities and put your energy into the area that you believe offers the best chance of achieving your goals.

- Do not dwell on unfairness from the past but always look forward.

- Carrying the right mental attitude will give you an advantage over the opposition, whether they are playing fair or not. It is important not to give your opposition a double advantage by mentally acknowledging defeat before an event has started.

- Only thorough mental and physical preparation will give you the confidence to beat your toughest rivals.

- There is no greater satisfaction than beating a suspected cheat.

- Every opponent has a weakness and cheating does not guarantee victory.

PART TWO

An important tumble-turn

1994

When a situation deteriorates you have the choice of staying with the formula of the past or making a change. Often the hardest part is recognising things are not going as planned and then acknowledging what went wrong.

My eyes were finally opened at the end of 1994. I was at a crossroad—remain the same or change. I wanted to be on the blocks in Atlanta ready to dive for gold and not watching the Olympics on television in my living room and wondering.

One positive in my favour was my perseverance and this remained a key part of my new formula. But just about everything else was adjusted in my rebirth. I changed not only the physical and mental preparation of my swimming but also my life out of the pool. I learnt to live a bit. My training was balanced with catching up with friends and having outside interests.

The main thing I learnt in this amazing tumble-turn of my life was that I had to believe in myself. I had to believe and visualise myself winning gold in Atlanta if I were to be the swimmer I had always aimed to be. I had made the choice to win.

2

CHAPTER FOUR

PERSEVERANCE

'Failure is only postponed success . . . the habit of persistence is the habit of victory.'

HERBERT KAUFMAN

'Always look to the front window screen rather than the rear-view mirror.'

UNKNOWN

An interesting Irish legend surrounds the famous Red Hand symbol of the O'Neills. According to the story, two chieftains, racing their boats to lay claim to the fertile land of Ulster in Northern Ireland, agreed that he who touched the shore first would gain possession of the lands. One of them, finding himself falling behind, cut off his right hand and hurled it ashore ahead of his rival. His claim to be the first to touch the shore was upheld and he was proclaimed the Prince of Ulster. The Red Hand is not just included on the O'Neills' shield of arms but it has become the symbol for the entire province of Ulster and its nine counties. I suppose you can say the will to win is in the O'Neill blood, but in my case it would defeat my purpose if I cut off my hand.

From a very young age I showed tremendous determination and focus, although I never aimed too high. Apparently when I was in Grade One I told the teacher I was not at school to play games but I was there to learn.

When I started making Australian stroke camps as a teenager I might have been shy but I still showed that O'Neill cheek. I would play charades to intimidate my rivals. I tried my hardest to beat everybody else and then when the training set was finished I tried not to look too puffed or tired. I was making out I didn't have to work hard to beat them when really I had been going at full boil. When they turned away I would inhale quickly to regain my breath. I was hoping to psych out my rivals so when I stood up to race them in competition there was no way they thought they could possibly beat me.

I may not have cut off my hand but I have made a lot of sacrifices for my swimming. I put my study on hold and had not had much of a social life, but I was happy to make those sacrifices to achieve success. By the end of 1994 I had achieved a certain degree of success as the owner of many international silver and bronze medals of which I was proud but I was starting to find it disheartening to be known as the perennial bridesmaid.

I felt for six years I had been the up-and-coming swimmer in the Australian team who had never made it. Six years is a long time to work at something and I felt frustrated I could not get past the minor medals. I knew I was capable of more. I was fed up being known as a 'pretty good' swimmer and, secretly, wanted to be the best in the world.

I clearly remember a youth camp I attended after the 1994 World Championships, where I addressed a group of school children. I was getting asked questions such as if I knew Kieren Perkins and Samantha Riley before I made the Australian team? Kieren and Sam deserved their high profiles and every reward that came their way after winning dual gold medals at the 1994 World Championships, but the questions compounded my frustration because I was on the Australian team two years before Sam and one year before Kieren. Then, leading to Atlanta, I received a letter from a school kid who was doing a project on somebody famous and she wrote to me only because Lisa Curry was not on the Australian team. In the letter she asked me questions about Lisa Curry, such as whether I knew her.

It was a difficult situation but I knew I could handle it in either two ways. I could cave in to the bridesmaid complex or I could fight so hard and earn people's respect and attention. I was never somebody who actively sought media coverage but at the same time I suppose I was searching for recognition after six years of reasonable success as an Australian representative. I knew it was something that really came back to me and how much I wanted to turn bronze and silver into gold.

For inspiration I had only to look to my own household, especially my father. He was so determined to become a doctor that when he was dating my mother he would limit her visits because they distracted him from his study. Fortunately my mother was very understanding. It took him 12 years in total to become a doctor and then an eye specialist, an ophthalmologist. It wasn't always an easy road and he often had to work second and third jobs when he was studying. He came from your average working-class family where both parents needed to work to put food on the table. He would sort mail at Southport Post Office in his university holidays which involved starting at 4 am. Another holiday job was collecting empty glasses at hotels. Then, when he was studying to be a specialist, he would come home after a day's work as a doctor and study for two or three hours at night, as most medical specialists have to do. I'm sure there were times when he felt like giving up but he showed all the qualities that a successful athlete, businessman or doctor needs. He showed that O'Neill determination, motivation and focus to achieve his gold medal.

I started swimming as a nine-year-old and was completing my twelfth year in the sport by the end of 1994. Like my father, I wanted to earn a masters degree with my swimming and also graduate with gold. My father had persevered for 12 years to achieve his ambition and I realised there was still time for me to do the same. Like my ancestors in the O'Neill legend, I was seeking my promised land and I wanted my hand to be the first to touch at the end of my race at the Atlanta Olympics.

NINE KEYS TO PERSEVERING

Generally I've never been someone who has examined my past in detail. I've always looked forward, never back. But at the end of 1994 I knew I had to make some serious analyses of what went wrong at the Commonwealth Games and World Championships. I wasn't happy with my swimming and I could no longer pretend that everything was right.

I've already mentioned in Chapter One how I detailed the areas I could improve, but I also found it helpful to list the things that had contributed to my swimming success. To obtain a full set of answers you need to look at both the positives and the negatives of a situation.

When you are looking at changing a formula it's important not to change everything. Often only a slight change is needed to an otherwise effective program. This is because with every success there is always an area in which things could have been done better and with every failure there is always a positive.

So I sat down and added up all the positives. I realised my biggest attribute was perseverance. I had overcome many self-doubts. I had not bowed to drug cheats. I had faced my swimming demons. I had conquered several burdens. And through all the trials and victories there was that one consistency – perseverance.

At the end of 1994 I was 21 years old and could just about qualify as a 'swimming grandma'. I had been in Australian teams for six years and was almost past my use-by date. In the past swimmers had retired young but swimming was changing. It had become a career which attracted corporate sponsorship and government assistance. Money has never been my main focus but I realised at the end of 1994 there were no financial restraints in stopping me from continuing to swim. The only thing stopping me from swimming was whether I still had that perseverance, the spirit and strength to continue to march on.

In looking at the positives I realised there were two keys to perseverance – to maintain an enjoyment and hunger in your work. The themes of enjoyment and hunger figured in just about every positive. Leaving out 1994 when I was not happy with my swimming and I seriously considered retiring, I have always enjoyed swimming and I have always had an incredible hunger to win. People talk about determination, motivation and discipline and these are all important factors but it is very difficult to succeed and make the necessary sacrifices if you don't find enjoyment in what you are doing and you don't have that hunger to continue to improve. Everything else will flow from those two themes. I realised that despite the confusion about my training situation, I still really enjoyed swimming and I was incredibly hungry for that Olympic gold medal. In fact, I had never been so hungry.

Here are my nine keys to persevering.

Self-motivation from a young age

Self-motivation is an important ingredient in any success story. Developing self-motivation from a young age will only help you in future years. Self-motivation usually comes from wanting to do something by yourself and not being pushed by anyone else. It is always a healthy sign when you are driven from within and your achievements are your own. Self-motivation usually means you are not only hungry to succeed but you are enjoying it, and by developing the trait from a young age you will gain a headstart.

Without realising it at the time, I was developing strong self-motivation under my coach Mr Wakefield. The biggest gift he gave me was a love of the sport. He never pushed the sport onto me and never pushed me in training. I believe a lot of 10-year-olds out there are being pushed. Put it this way, all the stars when I was 10 are not the ones that are around today. You wonder how much they were pushed and what effect it had on them.

In many ways Mr Wakefield was exactly the opposite because many swimmers could get away with cheating in training. I often came home upset after training when other swimmers left early because they marked off their times when they had not really done all the work. Some swimmers would lean on the rope or not swim full laps in training. It was frustrating when they wrote down a fast time at training and you knew the only reason they went fast was because they cheated. Others would make excuses and stop before the end of a hard set.

When my mum saw me upset I would explain what had happened in training and she would say, 'They are only cheating themselves'. This is a good way of looking at it. I can never remember Mr Wakefield really pushing me, he always put the situation back to me. Some call it intrinsic motivation because you really learnt how to motivate yourself and those who didn't, or cheated themselves, never made it. They all quit long ago because they had not developed self-motivation.

It was a good thing Mr Wakefield never pushed me when I was young. I swam because I wanted to be there and it was up to me to work out how determined I wanted to be. I was able to develop a real love of the sport at my own pace. Of course there came a time in 1994 when I needed outside motivation, but self-motivation was the foundation of what I needed to succeed.

A balanced focus

Success comes from balance. It becomes a matter of finding the right equilibrium, because an all-consuming focus can topple your goals. Many people overlook how important it is to have a balance in life with home, work and outside interests.

During my school years, both study and swimming shared my focus. In fact, school was probably my main focus and swimming was more of a sideline. But my schoolwork and swimming both helped each other. People who are good at sport are usually pretty good at school as well because you learn to manage your time well. I would come home from swimming every afternoon and then discipline myself to study most weeknights and weekends.

When you have two things in your life there is not so much pressure on either one. As the saying goes, not all my eggs were in the one basket. This helped me handle my 1988 Olympic disappointment. At the time I was not as upset as I could have been, because I had other things in my life such as school and my friends. I didn't feel the intensity and pressure with my swimming.

Swimming didn't become my main focus until I left school and it was then I had problems in finding a balance. It's important to have interests away from your main pursuit, otherwise your focus can become distorted.

Rung by rung

Always set realistic goals and aim at your level. It is amazing how, when you continue to concentrate on immediate goals and achievements, one day you will suddenly find yourself there at the big goal. Never set goals that seem too daunting because success is a gradual process, and you gain pleasure every time you take another step.

I kept a log book which helped me to see how much I had improved in each event when I was young. It's important to be able to see what level you are at and what you need to aim for to climb to the next rung. When I was young I didn't win heaps of medals, so by assessing my personal bests I was able to see how much I had improved. Don't compare your level with other people's levels and achievements. Everyone has a different speed at climbing the ladder. I didn't need medals or comparisons with other swimmers to know what rung I had reached. My personal improvement was the only tool I needed to measure my progress and assess my next goal.

The higher you climb the ladder the tougher it gets. When you start at something you will always make big gains, but it becomes harder to improve as you get better. You must keep going even when the going becomes more difficult. When I was young I didn't appreciate how special personal bests were and consequently there are some rungs harder to scale than others. Between 1987 and '88 I made a six-second improvement in the 100m butterfly, but now I would be happy to improve by one-tenth of a second in my events. So a step up the rung, no matter how small, always provides the satisfaction and enjoyment of advancing to a higher level. And that success makes you determined to keep climbing.

I was never a person who set really high goals, like one day representing Australia at the Olympics. If you set your sights for the top of the ladder and skip the rungs leading to the top, it becomes easy to lose the grip on your focus when the climb becomes too tough. So when I was 10 years old I didn't set my sights on the Olympics, it would have seemed impossible to reach. It ended up taking me another eight years to go to the Olympics and there were a lot of rungs to climb in those eight years. But by taking the climb in small steps, my focus remained on swimming. I could give 100 per cent when I could see my next rung was in reach.

When you are busy concentrating on your immediate goals you can sometimes be surprised at what level you have achieved. The small steps add up. When I came second at the 1988 Olympic trials as a 14-year-old it was a huge surprise. There was no way I would have thought I would be so high up the ladder, but suddenly I was good enough to represent Australia at the Olympics.

It's also important not to jump too quickly up the ladder. It's not healthy to win an Olympic gold medal at the start of your career because then you don't really appreciate what you have achieved. You miss out on the satisfaction of climbing each rung but, more importantly, you miss out on the true value of your achievement. You cannot savour the view from the top when you don't have the understanding of how hard each step was to reach it. When I reached the Olympic level I didn't forget about my climb to get there: I was able to enjoy the satisfaction-rung by rung.

Learning from example

Don't be afraid to learn from others because everybody has something to offer. Success is not measured by years and experience but by how quickly you are able to soak up the knowledge and wisdom from observing and learning from the people and environment around you. Success is a quality impossible to inherit but is achieved by committed and hard-working students of life.

It always upset me when people said I had an easy life and success had come easily for me. I suppose people make this presumption because I come from a high-achieving family. My father John is a medical specialist, my mother Trish is a nurse, my brother John is a doctor and my younger sister, Catherine, is studying medicine. People say to my parents how lucky they are to have such a successful family, but success has relatively little to do with luck or genes.

I was fortunate to have parents who led by example, who showed success only came from hard work. Everyone is born with talent in one or several fields but it is how you use that talent that matters. My parents never pushed us but we learnt from their example that if we wanted to get anywhere in life we had to work at it, that it wasn't going to fall in our laps. I never just happened to achieve in the pool and a doctor's degree never just fell at the feet of my father and brother.

I was also able to learn from my parents about a balanced outlook on life. Besides learning about the rewards of hard work they helped me to put swimming in perspective. I learnt whatever success I had in the pool made me no better than anybody else.

I know my family and friends are one of the main reasons why I still enjoy swimming, and they gave me a perfect environment to ensure success. My parents were never typical swimming parents. They never owned a stopwatch or walked up and down the sideline clocking my times. They never kept a tally of my personal best times or analysed every training session or race. Actually we rarely talked swimming at home but I knew I had my family's support because of the sacrifices they made. Mum drove me to training and looked after my meals and, as we only ever holidayed as a family, they waited until the Queensland swimming championships were finished in January.

I never felt pressure from my family or friends to perform. In fact, in many ways my family were the opposite. My mother would come to swimming carnivals and would often be chatting with other mothers when my race was on so she would miss half of it. I was lucky to have school friends who were supportive but never made a huge deal of my achievements so I felt like a normal person at school. My family and friends were always supportive but that support never became overbearing so I never saw swimming as an obligation. So I didn't have to search too far to find examples about the benefits of hard work, humility and support.

Quality not quantity

To remain at anything for a long time it is important to pace yourself. It's easy to fall into the trap that quantity is the answer and to over-train, which can lead to burnout. It takes more than a lot of training sessions to win. The main emphasis should be on how you prepare. A key to success is to use your resources smartly and efficiently, which results in quality work sessions.

This is a philosophy that is especially important when you are young or new at something. My main memory of swimming when I was little was of it being fun and something I loved to do. I wasn't doing as many sessions as a lot of my childhood rivals but I never felt I was off the pace in my age group, even when I went through that hard time as a 13-year-old in 1987 and almost quit.

When I finished second at the 1988 Olympic trials I was training less than most of my competitors, although training still started at 5.30 am and I trained every afternoon followed by fun sessions every Saturday morning. I began to train full-time during the winter when I was 15 years old. The quantity of sessions increased gradually and there was never a stage I felt overwhelmed by my workload.

Mr Wakefield was smart because all the work he gave me

was quality. Even though I was not doing the kilometres of other swimmers, the training he gave me still made me swim fast. He never pushed me too hard so I never got sick of training. But he was still able to make me appreciate going fast. And because Mr Wakefield concentrated on quality and didn't give me heaps of butterfly training I never suffered from an over-use or over-strain injury, which is quite common with butterfly swimmers.

Training changed as an 18-year-old when I decided to aim for the 200m butterfly. It became harder then because before training had been sprint-orientated, which I found easier. Obviously my training is much harder now but there is still an emphasis on quality work and I swim only what I can manage.

I had a perfect preparation for a career which has spanned 15 years and counting. If my emphasis was on quantity for all those years I would have got sick of it by now and retired. Instead, I was able to pace myself, which I believe is the key to longevity. But most importantly, I still enjoy the sport. Let's face it, it's hard to enjoy any activity when you are overburdened with long training hours from the start.

Regular competition

Everyone wants to achieve their goal and be at their best for a big event or competition. The key is to be prepared for your toughest challenge. So it makes sense to have competition in training or your daily work, which can only make you stronger and better prepare you for your big event.

Training is where the hard work is done and nothing will make you work harder than competition. You need a winning attitude for the daily grind to taste success at the end. Competition in training provides that extra stimulus in the days, weeks or months leading to a big event.

From an early age the daily challenge in training was to beat other swimmers, especially because most of them were older than me, helped me to improve and be at my best for championship races. I always trained better when I had somebody to race, and regular competition made me even more hungry for success. Use regular competition as a challenge to bring out the best in you.

Without competition in training I had no way of measuring how well I was progressing and I lacked a challenge. But as an elite athlete I am no different from anyone else who is pursuing a goal. Everybody needs challenges in their work as part of the process of improving. Competition always provides a challenge, and if you can regularly overcome challenges it will only make you stronger and better prepared for your biggest challenge.

Always give 100 per cent

I suppose this is an obvious tip, to always give 100 per cent, but no one has reached the top with half-hearted efforts. The most important thing to remember is that a 100 per cent effort should be given in training, in competition and in everyday life. If you work daily at always giving your best effort it will be a quality that will come naturally when you need it the most.

I think I was about 10 or 11 years old when I first appreciated the value of always giving 100 per cent. I was selected for the Pan Pacific school competition in Darwin and came third in my race. Up until then I had never really cared how I went. But I distinctly remember that meet because I knew I could have done better if I cared, and I realised I had not let just myself down but also my coach and family because I hadn't swum my best.

The worst thing was I couldn't change the result. I would never know if I would have won if I had given a 100 per cent effort. It always feels good when you win but after that race I recognised the satisfaction you can enjoy if you know you have swum your best. And that way you know you are never missing out on any opportunities. When you give 100 per cent effort to all parts of your life don't be surprised how often you are repaid with a win. At the least, by giving your best you are increasing your chances of success.

Fired by competition not reward

If you focus on the rewards it becomes easy to lose track of what you need to do to achieve them. So many people talk about wanting to win medals, of achieving that job promotion, or of becoming a millionaire, but the secret lies not in focusing on the result but on how you will get there. The reward should never be the motivation but competition should provide the challenge to achieve.

I was never somebody who focused on reaching a team, breaking a record or winning a certain number of medals, but I learnt the hard way when I did. The first time I really concentrated on making a team was at the 1990 Commonwealth Games and I was so tense and tired from worry I only just scraped into the team with times far from my personal best. Now I have learnt to focus on my swimming rather than skipping ahead to the reward. The only time I really aimed at winning medals, seven gold at the 1994 Commonwealth Games, it harmed my swimming. Obviously it is something everyone thinks about but I realised my main motivation always came from beating the opposition.

Competition always fired me up. If your main focus is to swim the best you can to win the race, then things like team berths, records and medals will come after that. I found I needed to be passionate and excited about swimming to swim well and that came from the challenge of competition. I could always swim a couple of seconds faster in competition than in training, in the same event in the same pool and under the same conditions. I am better at racing than training because competition provides a real challenge and I always want to finish first.

Winning medals and breaking records should never be the main focus in a race situation. They are just abstract motivations, because you cannot race a time or a team berth. Rather, they are distractions that will make you try too hard and put you under unnecessary pressure and tension. Competition will always be the best way of setting from point A to point B the fastest.

Never look back

The best way to go forward is to not look back. Every year provides different challenges and situations. You can learn from past experiences but don't spend time comparing yesterday and today in detail because you will become caught up in the past and lose your focus on the future.

Everybody is different and there are some athletes who keep detailed log books about how they felt and what has worked for them over the years. I have never questioned or worried too much about what we did in last year's training programs compared to this year. I have come to realise that what worked for me one year will not guarantee success the next year. So I have always looked through the front windscreen and not the rear-view mirror.

Sometimes unavoidable obstacles, such as injuries, happen, and you have to change your training. If you are stuck on the same formula it becomes hard to adapt to a new schedule. I've found you are never the same athlete from one year to the next. You are continually changing and developing and every year your opposition brings new challenges. So I focus on the present to be prepared for the future.

I've never been someone who's been intense about the details of my swimming career. I have no idea how many Australian titles I've won. I've never really analysed my times and my competitors' times from last year to this year. Some people know every competitor's best times and that knowledge motivates them, but that has never worked for me. I prefer to concentrate on training hard and leave the analysis to my coach. I want to enjoy swimming and too much analysis can make it stressful. It's not healthy to be constantly sweating on competition times and training detail because there's a danger it could take over your whole life. I spend so much time training and working hard with my swimming that in my spare time I just want to switch off. I've simply concentrated on what I had to do to get ahead and have left the details of my past for others to worry about.

PRACTICAL TIPS FOR YOUR BIG EVENT

I've been in Australian teams since 1989 and over the years I've collected some invaluable practical tips. Many of them come from the practical advice given to me by the man who coached me in my first few Australian teams, Ken Wood. Obviously the tips are swimming-orientated but they could be easily applied to anyone preparing for a big presentation, an important exam or a major competition.

1. Always keep your focus in preparation: your focus needs to be just as strong in preparation as for the event itself.
2. Cover all physical bases: you can ask for no better preparation start than if you are healthy.
3. Break up events into parts: success becomes more digestible when events are broken into parts because small improvements add up to big improvements.
4. Concentrate on the task and not the finish: you will get to a place faster only if you keep your mind on doing the best you can on the present task.

CHAPTER
FOCUS

- Perseverance comes from enjoyment of your activity and a hunger to succeed.

- Your focus should always be balanced.

- Set realistic goals.

- Don't be afraid to learn from others.

- Make sure your preparation is quality not quantity.

- Competition is a great motivator.

- Always give 100 per cent.

- Be fired by competition and not reward.

- Never look back.

CHAPTER FIVE

CROSSROADS

'There is the point of no return where you have laboured so long, sacrificed so much, that you can't go back. You must reach your goal and trample on anyone who tries to stop you.' **HERB ELLIOTT**

'I will go anywhere – provided it be forward.'
DAVID LIVINGSTONE

'**Undoubtedly the high point of your swim career to date** . . . What lies in the future? It's exciting just to contemplate. The Best in the World?'

Mr Wakefield wrote this in a 1992 diary he kept on my career. He kept a résumé on many of his swimmers and each year he recorded the times for all the competitions and he wrote a comment on the year. Looking back, the statement was prophetic for several reasons. Frustratingly for me, my bronze medal swim at the 1992 Barcelona Olympic Games remained my high point for the following three years. I felt trapped, stuck in that golden summer day in Spain. I had not been able to break out of the time warp and take a step forward. But more importantly, 1992 was the high point in the coaching and pupil partnership between Mr Wakefield and myself. By staying with Mr Wakefield I felt glued to the past.

No relationship is free from testing times and only the strongest survive. The years 1992 to 1994 were the test of our relationship. I had been with Mr Wakefield for 12 years and for the first 10 years all we did was move forward. When we came to a pothole we were able to move up a gear or change course. But then suddenly came the trough, a trough so big it threatened to swallow my career and our partnership. It remained uncertain whether I would climb out of it alone, together with Mr Wakefield or never.

By 1994 I knew I was coming to a crossroad, facing a fork with four prongs–to change sport, to change coaches, to retire and change career or to remain the same. The most difficult part is to recognise the crossroad when it comes. To know when to change and what option to choose.

The idea of change was not new. It was something I had tentatively been playing around with in my head since mid-1993 when the AIS had made overtures about a scholarship. But by the end of 1994 I knew I had well and truly found my crossroad.

Before the 1994 Commonwealth Games the thought that this could be my last year in swimming was very strong and changing coaches was not something I seriously contemplated. My thinking was more along the lines of if I were to finish with Mr Wakefield I would finish with the sport for good. I suppose it was difficult for me to imagine swimming without Mr Wakefield. But after my disappointing Commonwealth Games I found the heavy weight of doubt lifted. I knew then I could no longer deny to myself I had to leave Mr Wakefield.

On the last night of the swimming competition at the Games while I was attempting to get some sleep I tried to imagine myself returning to Mr Wakefield's squad. It was amazing because I could no longer see myself turning up to training at the Chandler pool. I could no longer see myself swimming up and down my private lane in lonely contemplation. Suddenly the thought of going back to Mr Wakefield's squad gave me an awful empty feeling in my stomach.

It was true I was swimming the worst of my career but really the important factor was that I no longer enjoyed the sport. If I could enjoy swimming again who knows what was possible? I just knew I could not go back to Mr Wakefield.

The Commonwealth Games was really the final clincher. Maybe because I felt I had reached the bottom and I felt things could not get worse. Maybe it also helped that I was out of my usual environment and new situations always bring new angles to problems. At the time I hated the 1994 Commonwealth Games but now I can see that in many ways it was a relief to fail. I mean, how could a swimmer who had won seven Commonwealth Games gold medals have left their coach? My failures made me really look at my swimming and it gave me the final push to make that change.

I realised the hard part is making the decision. Once I had decided I needed a change I was the most motivated I had been all year. It seemed everyone had been on a huge high after

Australia had won a record 24 swimming gold medals at the Commonwealth Games. So it was natural many experienced a letdown after such an emotional and exciting Games, except me. Now there was a clearer path for my future. I no longer lacked motivation because I wanted to prove to myself I could swim faster at the 1994 World Championships. I wanted to show I was better than the sluggish and confused swimmer who took my place at the Games.

In both the 100m and 200m butterfly at the World Championships I finished behind two Chinese but because I was going through such a monumental tumble-turn in my career at the time that was only really a minor consideration. I knew I needed to sort myself out first before I worried about my opposition.

Again there was relief when I won bronze and not gold because it would have been very difficult to leave a world champion coach. It is funny to think I was probably less than two seconds, the margin between gold and bronze, from deciding whether I would leave Mr Wakefield. Even so, thoughts about retiring still occupied the plans for my future because I had lost so much confidence and I doubted I could go faster.

After the 1992 Olympics Mr Wakefield and I had been gradually growing apart. During 1994 I could easily go to training and not talk to him for a whole session as I followed the same program of the year before and the year before that. So when failure came at the Commonwealth Games neither of us knew how to handle it. These situations often draw people together and make a relationship stronger, but it was only when Mr Wakefield and I did fall into the trough that I realised we had just grown too far apart.

I never blamed Mr Wakefield for my not swimming well but it had reached a point where I wanted to get on with my future. After making the decision to leave Mr Wakefield I recorded improved performances at the World Championships so I came back from overseas knowing there was a good chance my swimming career could be rescued but that nothing could save my relationship with Mr Wakefield. I knew swimming the same routine at the same pool would remind me too much of my recent failures. I knew no matter how many changes Mr Wakefield made to my program, it could not stop the fact that for me to move forward with swimming, I needed to change coaches.

It is so hard to make a real career-changing decision but often it is just as hard to put your changes in action. Both processes take a lot of courage. I went down to the Gold Coast a few times and stayed with my cousin at Surfers Paradise. I found escaping to the coast and surfing cleared my thoughts and helped me gain the courage to leave Mr Wakefield, but for almost a month I couldn't bring myself to tell him that I wanted to leave him. I remember telling him a few times that I had some doubts about swimming and I was thinking about trying surfing or surf lifesaving or that I was going to try different squads for a couple of weeks, including Dennis Cotterell's and Scott Volkers'.

Retiring was an option because I kept thinking I could go back to university and earn a degree and so then in a few years' time I would be a professional with a stable career, which swimming was not. That was a pretty enticing option for a 21-year-old. In some ways I had felt my life was on hold while I was swimming. But then I knew if I retired I would always wonder how I would have gone at the 1996 Olympics and whether that gold medal would have been mine. Every athlete wants to leave the sporting stage on a high note.

So options were swirling around in my head but as the days went by I realised moving to another coach was the answer. But my future wasn't permanent until I cut the ties with my past and told Mr Wakefield it was over.

The media found out about one of my trials with Dennis Cotterell on the Gold Coast. Suddenly I was front-page sports news and photographers were hiding in the bushes to get a photograph of me at the Miami pool. Then journalists rang Mr Wakefield and he told them there was no doubt I would never leave him.

After a month of working up courage, the publicity forced my hand. I knew I had to sort it out with Mr Wakefield before it turned into a public drama. I went to his house the next afternoon and I was red-eyed when I told him I was leaving him. I'd always been able to hold back the tears in front of him but in privacy I had a few cries about the dilemma. He was very good about it, his only negative comment was to tell me I had made a mistake. He told me no one had ever improved who had left him. But that was the best thing he could have said to me because it fired my determination to prove that prediction wrong.

Leaving Mr Wakefield was the toughest thing I've ever done. I know I am only in my twenties so I'm sure there will be harder tests in the future, but up to this point it definitely has been my hardest act. Once I actually told Mr Wakefield, all the heavy weight of uncertainty was lifted off my shoulders.

It was such a hard decision because I realised it was the first time in my life I would be deliberately upsetting somebody. Whatever I decided, somebody would get hurt. I was very conscious of the value of loyalty. I had been with Mr Wakefield for 12 years and had grown up with him, he was like a grandfather to me. He had put a lot of work into me and I really appreciated that. I know I could not have won an Olympic bronze medal without him. How could I dare leave him?

Ironically, a big source of my courage to leave was a quote Mr Wakefield had given me several years before to put in my log book. It was about not letting anyone stand in your way to achieving success. The quote sounds harsh but it made me realise no matter how harsh my decision was, I had to do what I thought was best for me if I didn't want to have regrets with my swimming. If I wanted to turn bronze medals into gold.

The quote made me realise I had trained for years and years and had made many sacrifices and I wanted to give winning an Olympic gold medal everything I could. I learnt that for me to achieve an Olympic gold medal there were times I had to be selfish, a concept that is hard to deal with. I learnt an Olympic gold medal could come at a price, such as hurting people.

In making such a tough decision I learnt I had to follow my head and not my heart. I looked at things rationally, without letting my feelings come into play. I had to base my decision looking towards the Atlanta Olympics and even beyond and not just on the next fortnight. I realised too much was at stake to let my emotions rule.

It came down to me not wanting to watch the 200m butterfly final from a lounge room but wanting to be ready on the blocks in Atlanta. It is hypothetical to wonder whether I would have won a gold medal if I had stayed with Mr Wakefield, but I had come to believe our relationship had reached a plateau.

So when I faced my crossroad I based my decision on belief and my own sanity. I realised the most important person in my decision was myself. I couldn't stay with Mr Wakefield because I'd lost my motivation with swimming and I was struggling with boredom and lack of self-confidence. No matter who my coach was I needed a change of environment. It would have been nice to stay with Mr Wakefield because he is a really lovely person, but I couldn't see myself winning a gold medal with him.

MAKING THE CHOICE AT THE CROSSROAD

Everyone faces a crossroad at some time in their life, often several. Whether it is to do with relationships, work or everyday issues such as moving house or whether to go on a diet. The crossroad marks a time of deep uncertainty and it is only when you make a decision that you can move forward. And when you do make a decision there is no guarantee it is the right one.

I am a terrible decision maker because there is so much risk involved. I have always had a lot of self-doubt and when I was at the crossroad all my doubts were exposed. In 1994 I learnt every decision carried doubts and fears of future implications. It was just a matter of me weighing up the positives and negatives of each decision. Most importantly, I had to focus on my priority which was to be mentally strong and in the right environment for my challenge of an Olympic gold.

When you make the decision it is important you embrace it with belief. If you believe you have made the right decision then it most likely will be the right decision. It took two unhappy years for me to realise I had reached my crossroad. These are the questions I asked when I was on my way to the crossroad, when I stood on the edge of uncertainty and chose to win.

Weighing up the good times

Often the best decision is to stay with what you have. The main drawcard in staying the same are the memories of the good times. It becomes a matter of how relevant those memories are for your future and how much work is involved in making sure the good times continue.

My happy and successful past with Mr Wakefield was the main reason I considered staying with him. He had made swimming fun for me and he had given me the gift of loving the sport. I started training at the Hibiscus pool when I was nine years old and I trained there for nine years. Before training we would either play touch-football, throw around a frisbee or jump on the trampoline so then doing the hard training sets didn't seem such a burden. Even now when I drive past the pool I sometimes feel like crying because I have so many happy memories of training and playing there.

But then the last three years with Mr Wakefield training became a chore and that is when I had to face change. By the end of 1994 I realised despite all the happy memories, they could not guarantee a successful future. I could no longer continue living on a once-happy past and I had to start looking to the future.

Assessing the problem times

A crossroad usually follows unhappy and problematic times. When things are going well and smoothly the direction is clear, just keep on going forward. When things are not working it's natural to seek a solution but it becomes difficult when none of the solutions seems natural and instead there's a confusing array of options. A crossroad can be permanent or temporary, it's a matter of assessing the depth of the problems. It seemed certain things would continue to sail ahead in 1992 after 10 years of happiness and hard work with Mr Wakefield paid off with a bronze medal at the Barcelona Olympics. There was clearly just one direction, forward.

Then more than two years of disappointment, doubt and unhappiness followed and I realised I had to assess my training and I identified several problems. I firstly looked at my environment. I missed the outdoors venue. Mr Wakefield had moved our base to the Chandler Aquatic Centre, which seemed such a dull and serious place to train in comparison. This change had contributed to me no longer finding swimming enjoyable. I also realised I had to return to a squad environment. Since the early 1990s I no longer had anybody to really push me in training and this was one of the reasons why I went downhill. It's hard to swim fast in competition when you are not swimming fast in training.

I also needed a change in training because my program had remained the same for the past three years, which was one of the reasons I felt stale and sick of swimming. Finally, I always believed Mr Wakefield and I had a close relationship until the swimming disappointments between 1992 and '94. At the 1994

Commonwealth Games I don't think he knew how to console me when I was swimming badly, and we didn't know what to say to each other. Then, when I was going through so much personal anguish with my future, I needed some personal space which I don't think Mr Wakefield realised. I think he was trying to overcompensate after the double blow of failure in 1994 and a deteriorating relationship. We had always been cordial to each other but there never was a deep communication and understanding between us and this lacking was exposed during the turmoil of 1994.

So, after I identified the problems at the end of 1994, I could no longer deny to myself the problems were stopping me from improving. Without Mr Wakefield's support and coaching I would not be where I am today, but training with him was no longer working and, more importantly, I couldn't see it working in the future.

In my assessment the problems were just too difficult to overcome. I needed that something extra to reach my potential. In the end I realised my only chance of success would come from a change.

Dealing with temptations

Temptations are often scattered along the path to the crossroad, which may make you turn off too soon from your journey to success. With every temptation, always weigh up the situation and if you cannot tell yourself why you should follow that path then don't change direction. You arrive at a crossroad when you are ready to assess the problems of your past and the needs of your future.

One of my temptations was the chance of a scholarship at the Australian Institute of Sport in 1993. When I was involved in an Australian sprint camp in Hawaii in 1993, coach Genardy Touretsky invited me on an AIS tour of Europe later that year. At the time I denied to the media I was considering moving permanently to the AIS, but I was really only a day away from moving. I was impressed with Genardy and his swimmer, dual Olympic gold medallist Alex Popov. They were a successful and confident pair and Genardy seemed interested in my career. I'm sure Genardy knew I was interested in training with him but it never came to the stage of formal negotiations. Instead, he offered me the chance to train with them for several weeks in Canberra and any assistance myself or Mr Wakefield wanted.

Moving to the AIS was certainly a temptation I thought long and hard about because Genardy and Alex were so confident and seemed to have the answers I was looking for. I enjoyed training with them in Hawaii. The only thing that kept me from moving to the AIS was one day of contemplation. I sat down and really searched inside whether I thought it was the right move. When it came down to it I couldn't tell myself why I wanted to move to the AIS.

I knew things were not right with Mr Wakefield. I was unhappy and I needed a change, but with the AIS proposal I was just clutching at straws. I had not yet recognised my future direction so when the first option turned up it looked very tempting. But because I didn't know my direction I didn't know if it was the right option or not. Thankfully I obeyed my instincts and didn't blindly follow the temptation of the AIS. I hadn't yet reached my crossroad because I hadn't assessed the problems of my past and my needs for the future. I wasn't ready to change.

It was only later I realised I needed a squad environment of people my own age and a change in my training program which the AIS could offer. But those positives were outweighed by several negatives. Firstly I had never lived away from home and at 21 years of age I had become comfortable with several luxuries, including my freedom. I think I would have found the constraints of living at an institute too much. And second, I didn't want to leave my family and home environment.

Then, in 1994 when I was facing my crossroad, I experienced another temptation – surfing. Changing sports was a serious consideration. Becoming a professional ironwoman, a triathlete or a surfer were all options I entertained. As a former state junior surf-lifesaving champion, the professional ironwoman circuit was very appealing but surfing was also in my veins. I was a tomboy when I was young and as soon as my brother and male cousins started to surf I followed and became competent.

One day when I was down the coast surfing there was a surf competition on. I didn't enter it but I was surfing in the free surf area next to where the competition was being held. When I came back to shore I was approached by a man, who, it later turned out, was an expert from a surf magazine. He didn't know who I was when he told me I showed a natural ability as a surfer. He said I had the basic skills and with the right coaching I could go a long way. He said I should consider entering competitions and that surfing could become a career.

I have to admit the idea of travelling around the world's best beaches was very tempting but I realised it was not practical because I would have to move down the coast and I couldn't afford to do that financially. As just a part-time surfer there was no guarantee of success. After weighing up the facts I realised swimming was still my best chance of sporting success.

Seeking expert advice

When facing the crossroad often the best approach is expert advice. Don't be afraid to gather other people's opinions. The ultimate person you have to listen to is yourself, but it doesn't hurt to be surrounded and guided by the ideas and opinions of others. Answers rarely come from one source alone. When you have had a difficult past it is only a positive step to be able to talk about your future.

I came to the conclusion I needed a change of coaches by myself, but never in my life had I talked to so many people in my search for answers. Between the Commonwealth Games and the World Championships I talked to many of the other swimmers in the Australian team about their training environments. I was the one initiating the conversations about where I should go. Not one swimmer or coach came to me and said if things are going badly I think you should do this. Instead, and suddenly for the first time in my life, I was the one firing questions: What can I do? Where can I go? Do you like training where you are?

Once I started to talk about my future swimming became exciting again. It was especially reassuring when I realised I was not the only swimmer contemplating change. I linked up with Sydney-based Elli Overton who was also going through a difficult time and we supported each other.

I particularly remember having coffee with Andrew Baildon, Darren Lange, Elli, Sam Riley and Daniel Kowalski at Seattle one day during a break in the training camp before going to Rome for the World Championships. Elli and I asked Sam, who was coached by Scott Volkers, and Daniel, who then was with Dennis Cotterell, about their coaches and they both really endorsed them. I remember that day for being excited; I finally felt I was getting closer to some answers and moving forward again.

Often one person stands out as your confidant, someone you respect and trust. It has to be someone who you feel comfortable with in spilling your heartfelt thoughts to and someone who you could show your emotions in front of without feeling embarrassed. Australian head coach Don Talbot was a valuable shoulder, ear and tongue as he witnessed my tears, listened to my fears and then told me his thoughts.

I had gone to him in 1993 when the AIS had seemed so tempting and it was he who made me realise I didn't really know why I wanted to move to Canberra. Don told me I was not ready to leave my home and my family but that I should persevere with Mr Wakefield. Then, in 1994, he realised I was struggling with the difficult decision to leave Mr Wakefield. He understood how close I was to Mr Wakefield but he also understood I needed a new stimulus if I wanted to improve my swimming. Don recognised I had reached my crossroad and he helped give me the courage to move forward. I would have changed coaches without Don's advice but I needed that final reassurance I was on the right path.

Another valuable confidant came from an unlikely source in American coach John Trembly, who trained 1992 Olympic gold medallist Melvin Stewart. He comes to Australian swimming camps every year in September and I was always involved in the camps so I got to know him quite well. John was always very interesting to talk to and I also respected his opinion. At the 1994 camp, after the World Championships, I remember he looked at my stroke and he told me I was a 2:07 swimmer, two seconds faster than my personal best. He told me I was capable of swimming a lot faster. He said he didn't know what my coach was like but he sensed I needed a new environment. It was great to have an outsider take time out to listen to my problems and offer advice. He then followed this up by writing to me to see what I had decided.

Obviously you cannot take in all the advice you hear but you need to dissect what's relevant and to pinpoint your priorities. I've always tried to listen to as much wisdom as I could even though I probably discarded about 70 per cent of it. A past downfall was that I was unable to talk to people about my problems. I realised to be able to listen you have to first be able to talk. At the end of 1994 I learnt to talk to others about my doubts and fears. Talking to others, especially respected experts, only helped me find the answers after a disappointing and confusing two years. Ultimately it came to me and my priorities but I wouldn't have had the full picture without the contribution of all the people I talked to.

Making the final decision

Eventually you will know when you are ready to make the final decision. You can only make the right decision after weighing up the positives and negatives of each pathway of the crossroad; avoiding the potholes of temptation; riding the wheels of good advice; and then using your head and not your heart as a compass. Decision making is about discovery. You have to discover yourself and what you need before you can make the right long-term decision.

I had used my head and not my heart in realising I should stay swimming in Queensland and not be tempted by surfing or joining the AIS program. I had used my head and not my heart in making my decision to leave Mr Wakefield and now I had to do the same for the final decision – choosing my next coach. It seemed I had two options in Scott Volkers and Dennis Cotterell.

It was an extremely important decision because I needed the right person in what I saw then as my final chance at winning an Olympic gold medal. I spoke to and trained with Dennis and Scott to make sure I completed a thorough assessment before I made my decision. I chose Scott Volkers for three reasons.

Firstly, I needed a coach I could communicate with through the highs and lows. During the World Championships I spent some time with Scott on the bus rides to and from the pool in Rome. I never told him I was thinking of changing coaches but I think he could sense I was feeling down. I distinctly remember him telling me before my races that I had to be happy. He was joking around and trying to cheer me up. I appreciated his efforts and I realised he had the knack of lifting me when I was feeling depressed. I found I could talk to Scott and I felt I could relate to him.

Secondly, I really needed an enjoyable and stimulating training environment. Obviously it was a bonus that one of my best friends, Sam Riley, was trained by Scott and she encouraged me to come across. Then Elli Overton and Angie Kennedy came over, so it was great to train in a squad environment with swimmers of similar age and standard. It was also a good sign that Scott attracted elite swimmers. It meant many competitive sets in training, which could only make all of us go faster. The other plus was Scott mostly trained at the outdoors Valley pool.

Finally, the biggest attribute which impressed me about Scott was that he was just as excited as myself in the challenge of turning me into an Olympic gold medallist. While I was trying to rise from a career low, he was riding a career high. Sam had just won two world titles, the 100m and 200m breaststroke, and broken the 100m breaststroke world record. He came back wanting a new challenge and he found it in me. I think he liked the idea that I was already a swimmer who had come a long way under Mr Wakefield and there was a lot of risk attached to Scott taking me on.

There was only room for marginal improvement or massive failure because I had already achieved a high rung on the ladder. It was a huge challenge in helping me make that final rung. And Scott was wanting to have a go. I liked his positive and confident attitude.

From the moment I first talked to him about me moving to him, he had a lot of belief in my rebirth. When I first spoke to him he said he believed I had not yet reached my peak and there was improvement in me. This was the best thing I could hear because I had come to believe I had reached my final plateau. He was keen to work on my technique and to make sure I was never 'twiggy' at competitions and that I would never again die in the last lap of races.

One of Scott's strengths is his motivational quality and I realised motivation isn't a solo task but a team effort. I felt by going to Scott my dream to win an Olympic gold medal was not just mine but also his. No one can succeed on their own and I started my two-year quest for Atlanta backed by Scott's belief and his strong support network. Just by talking to Scott and deciding to join his squad I felt I had taken a big leap forward. I had regained my enjoyment of swimming and hunger for success, which became the first step in my quest for an Olympic gold medal.

AFTER THE CROSSROAD

When you make a major change in your life you should first analyse your options and then believe in your decision once it is made. But it is still important you set yourself tests. If your change has not been successful, don't be afraid to go back to the crossroad.

I was very nervous for my first session with Scott after 12 years with Mr Wakefield's squad, but from the start I came to Scott with the attitude of wanting to improve. I know everyone when they first change coaches nearly always improves. Maybe it has something to do with your ego and wanting to impress your new coach and also wanting to show other swimmers and coaches you have made the right decision. Fortunately for me, after the first week I knew Scott had provided all the attributes I was looking for.

Despite the instant success with Scott, I still set a couple of tests to check my decision. I realised my new-found enjoyment and hunger with training may just have been a temporary sensation and that I might lose that feeling after the excitement of a new change had worn off. But with Scott I continued to find training exciting, from the first day I arrived to now.

But the main test I set for the change to a new coach was the Queensland Swimming Championships in January, almost three months after moving to Scott in October. I surprised myself with my first personal best time in the 200m butterfly for almost three years. The change of coaches had passed the test with flying colours. It was a relief to know all the signs were there that my change looked a permanent success and not a fleeting one.

I had been weighed down with the thought of change for almost two years. I had suffered a lot of heartache and gone through a lot of painful soulsearching in the process. It was like a fairytale how straight away things went right when I came to Scott. But I'd spent a lot of time at the crossroad ensuring I took the right path. On the surface it looked like things had come easily for me under Scott but I'd brought both belief and a high work ethic to give my decision the best chance of success.

CHAPTER
FOCUS

- When you have to make a difficult decision, no matter how painful, abide by your self-belief and what is best for you.

- You can only make the right decision after weighing up the positives and negatives of each pathway of the crossroad.

- It is important to avoid the potholes of temptation. Do not be worried if you recognise the wrong option before the right one.

- Do not be afraid to ride the wheels of good advice.

- Use your head and not your heart as your compass at the crossroads.

- Decision making is about discovery. You have to discover your problems of the past and your future needs before you can make a decision.

- When you do decide on a path you have to bring both belief and a high work ethic to give the change the best chance of success. Be prepared to set tests or return to the crossroad to make sure you do find the right path.

CHAPTER SIX

BELIEF

'Your ability never changes, only your perception of your ability changes. It is learning to believe in your ability.'

GARY STICKLER (a coach of Pat Rafter who faxed this quote to him during his successful 1997 US Open campaign)

'You have to want to win and expect that you are going to win. Top players have that edge. Even if they're down a few games, they know they're going to come up with what it takes to win.' **MARTINA NAVRATILOVA**

Everybody has their moment of truth and mine came at the 1992 Barcelona Olympics. In 1992 my 200m butterfly Olympic bronze medal race was a celebration. By 1994 it had become a torment. In 1992 the race had put me on a career high. By 1994 it had become a major contributor to my career low.

At the time I was thrilled with an Olympic bronze medal but later I realised I had shrunk from my moment of truth. For 175 metres I had stared victory in the face as the race leader and then fear, uncertainty and doubt took over. I didn't believe I was a gold medallist. That race started to haunt me because I became known as a swimmer who 'died' in the final lap. I was somebody who couldn't finish strongly when it counted. I was somebody who didn't have that final strength and courage to surge to victory. It is not a flattering image for an athlete.

The race is still clear in my memory. I remember I was incredibly nervous in the marshalling area, maybe the most nervous I had ever been for a race. It was my first Olympics and the biggest race of my career. All my dreams of representing Australia at the Olympics were being realised at that moment.

My nerves seemed to multiply in the tense and stifling atmosphere of the marshalling area. There were many new faces in the final, including myself, so none of us really knew each other. Not knowing any of the other competitors didn't help my confidence and I remember trying to sit somewhere so I could be inconspicuous. The only competitors who broke the silence were the two Americans, who were loud and almost cocky in their manner. For an Olympic rookie I was pretty intimidated and in my nervous state I was fooled into believing a confident appearance out of the pool guaranteed success in the pool.

When there is silence it means there's nothing to distract your nerves. To further rattle my nerves I was sitting in the marshalling area as the fastest qualifier for the final. The enormity of the situation was quickly sinking in, especially when Australia was still seeking its first Olympic gold medal in the pool. The worst thing you can have before a race is uncontrolled nerves and that is exactly what I had as I marched out to take my position behind Lane Four.

Mr Wakefield had left me with only one instruction for my biggest race–to take it out and let the others chase. I stood on the block reciting 'Loose as a goose'. The gun went off and I dived in with those words on my lips. This was my saying to try to relax me and get me into a rhythm with my butterfly stroke, but nothing could make me relax.

I sprang out from the blocks and my nervous energy was released. All I knew was I had to take the lead, which I did for three laps. I had sprinted the first 100 metres under the 1981 world record pace. All I can remember thinking was how easy it felt. It was an unbelievable feeling as I rode on nervous energy.

I turned for the last lap in front and I started to think, Oh my God, I'm going to win a gold medal. I distinctly remember thinking, I'm going to win, I'm going to win. Then suddenly a grand piano seemed to land on my arms. I could barely raise my arms above the water and I felt like I was sinking. There was a burning feeling all over my body and the pain was intense. The final lap seemed to grind to slow motion as every stroke became an effort. I remember frame by frame as the Chinese swimmer, Xiahong Wang, and the American Summer Sanders came into view and then drew level. It was my moment of truth. Did I have the belief, courage and focus to take a stranglehold and finish the race as strongly as I had started it, or would I succumb to fear, uncertainty and doubt?

I was overtaken by pain and I felt so weak while Xiahong and Summer seemed to gather strength. In my depleted state I had convinced myself they were better swimmers than me and were going to pass me. Of course my fears were realised. As soon as I worried about others catching me I forgot about my own performance. As soon as I lost my focus, my future became uncertain.

And, finally, I doubted I could win a gold medal. In my moment of truth I didn't have the self-belief of an Olympic gold medallist. Now I realise a victory was impossible because I never had the courage nor the confidence to control the race. Instead, the race controlled me. Summer won in 2:08.67, Xiao-hong was second in 2:09.01 and I was third in 2:09.03. Incredibly, I had swum the second 100 metres almost eight seconds slower than the first 100 metres.

So instead of the focus being on my winning the bronze medal in my first Olympic Games, it seemed everyone talked about my 'dying' last lap when the gold medal slipped away. The seed of doubt that I died in races was planted in Barcelona and it kept growing and feeding on my increasingly low confidence until it matured and flowered in 1994. Another insecurity which started at Barcelona was my bad first days in competition. This doubt also continued through to 1994.

It's hard to know whether these factors, which developed into self-doubts, stemmed from a preparation or a mental fault, or maybe a mixture of both, but I know now the big difference between a bronze medal and a gold medal was my lack of self-belief. What fuelled my insecurities is that in every competition they were chronicled in media previews and reviews. It is difficult to deal with a private self-doubt but it can explode out of control once it becomes talked about in the media. Once so many people know about a performance fault or a technique weakness, you are regularly asked about them and they become the focus of attention rather than your positive points. The self-doubts can then grow in power until eventually you become convinced they are real, and when you enter races they are as much a part of you as your togs and goggles.

When you are confident everything comes easily and when

you are not performing the worries and self-doubts emerge. That is when you fall into the trap of over-analysing. Every fault and error doubles in size and then you start panicking about changing techniques and programs. Doubts such as 'I'm too old', 'I'm too unfit' or 'I've reached my peak' invade your mind and take over your focus. But when this inner struggle becomes a public event played out before the media circus then there is a danger the doubts will become uncontrollable.

It comes with the territory that the media will focus on the highs and lows of an athlete's career. Cricketer Mark Taylor and golfer Ian Baker-Finch have had their form slumps even more widely chronicled. My problem was that with little confidence and no self-belief the doubts about my race finish and bad first days of competition snowballed. I was very vulnerable and instead of ignoring the media stories, I started to believe what was being written and broadcast. By the end of 1994 I believed without question I died in the last lap of races and I always had bad days on the first day of competition. It came to such a low point that I even publicly acknowledged my weaknesses in interviews.

So I came to Scott Volkers at the end of 1994 with the heavy baggage of self-doubt. But at least I had realised what I needed to save my career – self-belief. I had worked hard and was determined to win at Barcelona but I didn't believe. Now for the 1996 Olympics in Atlanta I realised I needed more than just hard work and determination. I needed self-belief.

By the end of 1994 I was turning around my thinking about the 1992 200m butterfly Olympic final. The race was no longer a torment but had become a huge motivation. The thought motivated me to train every day. In 1992 I had become seen as a swimmer who 'died' in races but at the 1996 Olympics I wanted to be seen as a swimmer who finished strongly. I wanted to be armed with self-belief for my next moment of truth.

ACHIEVING SELF-BELIEF

Self-belief doesn't guarantee success but it is the most important component in any success story. If you don't believe you will win the race, if you don't believe you will get that sales project, if you don't believe you will lose 15 kilograms and if you don't believe you will pass that university exam, then you won't. To achieve a target you have to see yourself achieving it. Every molecule of your body has to believe. Without self-belief there is nothing to protect you from your self-doubts.

Australian head coach Don Talbot rates self-belief as so important that without it your chances of winning drop 80 per cent. He says if you have self-belief your chances of success increase by 75 per cent. No matter how much coaches, family and friends tell you that you will achieve your goal it will not make a difference until you yourself start believing. Your coaches, family and friends cannot compete for you, sit your exam, gain that important sales project or lose weight for you. Only you can make that difference and that difference comes from self-belief. Your ability remains unchanged. It is simply learning to believe in it.

Throughout my career coaches, family and friends had been telling me I could achieve the ultimate in sport but I never believed them. A strong lack of self-belief was the chink in my armour. It was why I couldn't see myself as an Olympian as a child; it was why I couldn't see myself beating Lisa Curry-Kenny at the 1990 Commonwealth Games; it was why I couldn't see myself winning the 1992 Olympic gold medal; and it was why I couldn't see myself beating the Chinese at the 1994 World Championships.

For me to win a gold medal at the 1996 Olympic Games I realised I had to go against my nature. A lack of self-belief was not a minor hiccup that could be fixed in a day. I knew it would be an intense 669-day war (from October 1994 to July 1996 at the Atlanta Olympics) against my most debilitating enemy – my own self-doubts.

The power of self-doubt is almost always underestimated. There is no more lethal enemy than self-doubt because it strikes from within and can reach more cracks in your make-up than any outside force. Because the battleground is within yourself it does not attract the attention from the outside but, believe me, the destruction and devastation is just as real. I've read about other athletes and their huge inner struggles and never equated it with my own private trials. But now I realise everyone's struggle with self-doubt is the same because the power of your enemy, your inner demons, never changes whether the battle is fought publicly, like Mark Taylor, or in privacy. For everybody, self-doubt is a silent enemy that moves by stealth. The damage it causes can be so deceptive that it goes unrecognised until years later.

By 1994 self-doubt had invaded every part of my body and the damage was now visible. After a year of failure, desperation and depression I was ready for the enormous task of reinforcing my many cracks with self-belief. Something usually triggers a regaining of self-belief and for me it was a change of coach and the challenge of the Atlanta Olympics. And no matter how famous a person is, the solution never changes: you have to look within to find that inner strength to start believing in yourself.

After my career low I had never been more hungry than now to win a gold medal. I knew if striving for Olympic glory did not help me achieve self-belief, then nothing would. Backed by a cause I was more than willing to fight for, I was determined my self-belief would triumph in Atlanta. I knew that for the 1996 Olympics I had to be in such a mindset that I could climb the blocks, gaze down the lane and believe I could win.

In my corner was Scott Volkers, who daily started to build up my battered self-belief. I had let myself become brainwashed by the media into believing I died on the final lap and I felt weak and sluggish on the first day of competition. These were the keys in building up my self-belief. So while I worked from within, Scott worked from the outside by improving my preparation, building up my confidence, making training enjoyable and stimulating and then correcting my weaknesses.

The first thing Scott told me when I moved to him was that I was never going to feel 'twiggy' and have a bad first day of competition again. I never did have a bad first day again. I had convinced myself I could never swim a strong final 50 metres but Scott told me I was never going to die at the end of my races again. And never again did a piano fall on me but instead I always felt strong on the final lap.

It was a huge risk to move to Scott less than two years before the Atlanta Olympics but it worked. It is hard to know how much my success had to do with a change of training and preparation and how much my new-found mental strength was a factor. But with Scott I had one big advantage – I always believed I was going to swim faster.

I have come to realise talent and a high work ethic will get you only so far. There are other people in Australia and around the world with a similar amount of talent who probably train just as hard producing comparable training times. Yet when I race them I know now I can beat them. It comes back to self-belief.

The best way to gain self-belief is to be the best prepared that you possibly can, which will give you more confidence. Training as hard as you can is another important factor. You know you have achieved self-belief when you quietly and calmly believe you are the best and no one else can beat you. So with 25 metres to go in a race you know you can win because no one else has trained as hard or prepared as well as you to answer the moment of truth.

Following is the 10-point plan I used with Scott to help me achieve my self-belief. I found it especially helpful because so much information concentrates on the practical side of success, such as technique and fitness, but you cannot win without mental strength. This formula helped me to exercise my belief and confidence and I still turn back to it for guidance because building and finetuning self-belief is a never-ending process.

Analyse weakness

Every situation or performance has a weakness but look upon it as a bonus rather than a burden. It means there is an area which can be improved and the thought of improvement only gives hope. The first step to success is to identify your weakness because you cannot start improving until you start to strengthen your weakness.

Initially Scott made a thorough evaluation of my performance. He especially concentrated on the 1994 Commonwealth Games and World Championships. My weaknesses were obvious but Scott looked beyond them. He looked at everything from physical faults, such as technique, to mental weaknesses, like believing my self-doubts. He identified and corrected the bad habits that had crept into my freestyle and butterfly strokes during the past few years. We worked on my slow turns. If I could pick up one-tenth of a second or more in each turn I would be half a second faster over the race.

The saying you are only as good as your weakest link is so true. I was only as good as my dying final laps and all my other weaknesses and until I started to improve those I was never going to be an Olympic gold medallist. My weaknesses fed my self-doubts, and they were a major hurdle to achieving self-belief. I had to turn my weaknesses into my strengths if I wanted to develop the self-belief of an Olympic champion.

Thorough preparation

Nothing contributes more to self-belief than a thorough preparation. There is no better feeling than when you approach a challenge knowing every aspect has been analysed and nothing more could be done with your preparation. By thoroughly covering your preparation you have achieved the foundation for not only self-belief but success.

My preparation for swimming had become a big problem and I no longer had confidence in my preparation. It's hard to believe you can win when you have niggling self-doubts about your preparation. When I went to Scott I was looking for the security of a strong preparation.

In swimming we have a taper, when in the final weeks before a competition we start a series of easy training sets to make us fresh for the competition. Scott completely changed my taper. I no longer did as many sprints but instead did more broken 200m butterfly races when I simulated my race. I would swim the first 50 metres in a similar time I wanted to complete my first 50 metres in the race and at the same time I would rehearse how I wanted to feel in the first 50 metres. For example, for my first 50 metres I wanted to feel easy and strong. Then I would have a 30-second rest and swim the second 50 metres in the time I aimed for, practising the correct feelings, followed by another 30-second break. Then I'd swim my third 50 metres, have another break and then the final 50 metres with the corresponding feeling of concentrating on my stroke and not sprinting to the wall.

I had been with Scott for just over two months at my first competition, the Queensland Championships, and using this different preparation I set a personal best in the 200m butterfly. It was my first personal best in the event since the 1992 Olympics. In such a short amount of time under Scott I doubt whether I would have gained a significant level of fitness and that the new training would have had time to take effect. In that two-month period the only major difference was a new preparation with my taper and increased self-belief.

It is often hard to know if you have had the right preparation until you have raced. All you can do is complete the best preparation you can and have full faith in your coach or adviser and then it becomes a matter of trial and error. It doesn't hurt to make the preparation harder than your actual challenge so when you do have to perform, it seems simple compared to your preparation.

In the two years leading to Atlanta my preparation was so draining and difficult that the race seemed easy compared with training. When you finish your preparation with the feeling that you could withstand the toughest test then it becomes another building block in your tower of self-belief.

Stimulated environment

One of the most damaging forces stopping self-belief is boredom. It is difficult to motivate yourself to be the best if you are bored with your work environment. A stimulating and fun environment makes work enjoyable and pushes you to do your best. You can only gain self-belief if you want to do your best.

By the end of 1994 it was no secret I needed new stimulus with my training. I moved to Scott because I wanted to enjoy my sport again and to be in a more competitive environment with a squad. With Sam, Elli, Angie and myself all training at a high level then training became stimulating on a daily basis. Suddenly I found I was enjoying training again.

Scott tried hard to keep us interested in training. Sam, Elli and I had been training for many years so we sometimes needed a change of program to keep us fresh and motivated. Sometimes we played games as part of training, like one time I did a handicap race against Sam. She swam a 200m breaststroke and then I had a 15-second handicap and I had to chase her with my 200m butterfly. Another time we had maximum effort sets and Scott turned it into a horse race format and gave everyone different odds which he wrote on the board.

Sometimes he joked around at training. Other times he was

really strict. He also uses a lot of different appliances to give us variety with our training, such as kickboards and paddles. Environment is so important. You have to enjoy being at work so you can produce your best. People always ask me how I keep training day after day doing the same thing, following that black line. But honestly, leading to the 1996 Atlanta Olympics I rarely found training boring. I was training for my goal and the stimulating environment of Scott's squad kept me mentally and physically fresh. A training environment that pushes you to do your best will only help you produce your best for your greatest challenge.

Be happy

Never underestimate the importance of being happy. A happy person often has the confidence to meet any challenge and then self-belief becomes a reachable stepping stone.

I had been plagued by moments of depression and I was not leading a happy and balanced life before I moved to Scott. None of this helped my swimming. When I moved to Scott I certainly became a lot happier with my swimming but there were also benefits outside the pool. Sam, Elli and I are close friends and we often had coffee or dinner after training though we rarely talked swimming away from the pool. So my life was becoming more balanced. I was starting to socialise and to have outside interests, such as surfing. I was starting to enjoy life again. This balance helped me enjoy my swimming again and achieve the right frame of mind for success.

Scott has always believed happy swimmers are fast swimmers. I know I have always swum my best races when I was happy because being happy and being confident go hand in hand. Obviously you are not going to be happy and in a good mood 100 per cent of the time and Scott was conscious of when we hit a downer. He would try to pick us up because he knew we had better training sessions when we were happy.

I did my best training sessions when I was happy. Whenever I wasn't in a good mood and I didn't want to be at training I tried to turn things around. I'd think about my goal of winning an Olympic gold medal, which always gave me a boost. I would also wonder what else I could do that I would enjoy as much as swimming. My answer was always 'Nothing'. It made me realise how much I enjoyed swimming. Being happy helped me to race and train well, which lifted my confidence and increased my self-belief.

Self-focus

It is natural to want to compare yourself to others but self-belief comes only from a self-focus. Comparisons with others often bring doubts about your own progress. The best way to develop self-belief is to develop tunnel vision and concentrate only on what you have to do to achieve.

With all my races I was conscious of my opposition. Throughout the race I monitored the progress of other swimmers. It became a factor of my swimming when I started to compete internationally in 1989. I knew I had to race the Americans and they seemed so good so I was constantly aware of them in my races. The more I thought about swimmers from other countries the more I became intimidated by them and the more I doubted my own ability. It wasn't until I moved to Scott that I realised this was detrimental to my self-confidence.

Scott started to develop my self-focus. He told me to concentrate only on myself in races, that no matter how overwhelming my competition appeared there was nothing that helped me to beat them by thinking about them. He said it was a waste of my time and energy, especially in the crucial minutes before and during a race. There was nothing I could do to slow down my opposition or make them disappear but the only path to self-belief and success was to improve myself.

Scott then told me all he could ask from me was my best and

this really honed my skill of self-focus. When you are self-focussed, instead of trying to beat this person and that person you are so busy concentrating on doing your best that suddenly you find yourself achieving your goals. I realised the only way I could start to gain self-belief was to concentrate on what I needed to do to win.

Change negative to positive

It's easy for negative thoughts to slip into your mind, and negativity breeds self-doubt. The most positive thought is to concentrate on doing your present task properly. If you are totally focused on your current challenge there is no room for negativity. Being positive is an important step in achieving self-belief.

When I turned, in front, for the final lap in the 200m butterfly at the 1992 Olympics, my thoughts were ruled by negativity. I was thinking that I couldn't let the other swimmers pass me and I couldn't die at the end of the race. Which is exactly what happened. And when I was passed it added to my negative thoughts because I naturally felt I was swimming slower. If you are passed, you automatically feel slower. And when you feel slow you not only start to feel the pain, but more importantly, you start to doubt yourself.

Scott helped me to think positively in races without me realising it. He helped me to blow away those negative thoughts. Scott told me to think about keeping my stroke long and smooth. He told me to focus on those black Ts at the end of the pool. He told me to concentrate on my breathing. I found I was so busy thinking about what I had to do to win the race I didn't have time to think about all the negative things that could happen. It also helped to take my mind off the pain you experience at the end of a race. It's always more positive to concentrate on what is happening, rather than any negative things which could happen.

This is something which is really hard to achieve, especially if you are not fully focused on your challenge. I sometimes still struggle with negative thoughts because for such a long time they ruled my races and were a major factor in my lack of self-belief. Keeping my focus totally on my task is something I will always have to work at so that one day negative-free races will become a natural process.

This is not just a tool for racing. I use it constantly with training, especially in the sessions that are very demanding and painful. Scott yells out 'Concentrate on your stroke' and when you start to do that it really does take your mind off your hurting arms. The more I practised turning a negative into a positive the stronger my self-belief became.

Finding pleasure in pain

The old saying 'No pain, no gain' is very true. If you find a challenge is painful then it usually means you are on the right track to success. When pain comes, always find motivation in the pleasure from a successful outcome. Self-belief comes from having the courage to break through the pain barrier.

The 200m butterfly is known to be one of the most painful races in the swimming program, especially the last 50 metres. By the end of 1994 I had started to dread racing the 200m butterfly because I knew in the last 50 metres my arms would start to hurt. Then when you start to concentrate on people passing you, it seems to become even more painful.

Scott taught me to feel pleasure in pain. He said, 'Imagine how good it would feel once you touched the wall first and then to turn around and see your name as the gold medallist. The pain would then be worth it.' To help us become familiar with pain and to push the pain barrier Scott regularly drove us hard in training. Then I started to think if I could survive so much pain in training it would help me swim faster when the race day came. Gaining the ability to work through pain paid off in the long run because the pain I experienced in my races was nothing compared with training. The race day seemed so easy in comparison.

Another tool Scott used to help build up my pain barrier was to conduct race simulation with our regular training runs through Brisbane city. He would compare the steep hill at the end of our running course to the end of my race. He would tell me to pretend it was the last 50 metres of my race and that I should relax and feel strong. But most importantly, he told me to enjoy the pain. I started to enjoy that pain in working hard to climb the hill because I could imagine the feeling of satisfaction and victory once I reached the top. I became familiar with the pain associated with reaching and then enjoying the spoils of being at the top of my mountain – an Olympic gold medal.

If something was easy then everyone would do it. Achievements like Olympic gold medals come only from hard work. If you want to achieve something special you have to realise pain comes in the parcel of success. There is nothing more satisfying than pushing through the pain barrier to gain victory. It is an achievement that builds self-belief.

Always aim at improvement

If you have only one goal in your life then it should be to improve. Nothing is more positive than the thought of wanting to improve. There is nothing more powerful at building self-belief than the knowledge you have done something better than you have ever done before. And striving for, and achieving, improvement will drive you further away from self-doubt and closer to self-belief.

Several years ago at training American-born Tracy Stockwell (nee Caulkins), a three-time Olympic gold medallist in 1984, gave us a lecture I will never forget. She told us that in every training session she tried to improve on something. If she hadn't bettered a training time then she aimed to dry herself better than ever before. The thought that drying yourself down well could one day lead to an Olympic gold medal may sound silly but if you think about it, always striving for personal bests is a great habit to master. And by breaking your goals down to small improvements your focus is kept on the present and you are not being distracted.

If in every session you are trying your best then one day the small improvements will add up. No matter how small the improvement, the thought and act of improving will only push you forward. The small improvements I tried for daily in training provided the best path to an Olympic gold medal.

The important thing to remember about the aim of improvement is that nothing is perfect and everything can be improved. You can never run out of goals. Every part of my race, including my start, my turns, my finish and my technique, could be improved. Once I may have seen this as a negative and it could have triggered self-doubts but now I see it only as a positive. The more room you have to improve, the greater the hope for success.

It is the best feeling when you swim faster than ever before because you know you are on the upward curve. When I achieved my first personal best in three years in the 200m butterfly at the 1995 Queensland Championships it did wonders for my self-belief because suddenly I saw myself marching forward again. There is no greater satisfaction and no greater builder of self-belief than improvement.

Positive feedback

Everybody has days when they are unmotivated and lethargic. It is impossible to be at your best every day, but positive feedback is the best way of keeping people on track with motivation and belief. Positive feedback is one of the best tools for building confidence and self-belief. Everyone needs to hear once in a while if they have done something good. Scott always made an effort to tell me if I had done something well.

When I was in the middle of a hard and demanding training set it always gave me a boost to receive some positive feedback. It took just a simple word of encouragement from Scott to motivate me. For example, one day he said to me I was the only person in the world to do this special training set and that gave me a real lift for the rest of the training session.

It was also reassuring to know Scott was monitoring all my sets. I have always excelled at self-motivation but with Scott I knew I was no longer on my own. It is impossible to be able to motivate yourself all the time and everybody needs a helping hand occasionally. With Scott's positive feedback I didn't feel alone in my battle to achieve the self-belief to win an Olympic gold medal.

Expect best performance daily

One of the biggest keys in achieving self-belief is to know you can always be successful when it counts, and the only way to have a high rate of success in big events or competitions is to expect your best performance daily. By constantly performing at your top level you come to expect what you once dreamt about achieving.

The concept of being able to perform your best anywhere and at any time first came to my attention at the Australian sprint squad camp in Hawaii in 1993. I was amazed to see Alex Popov come close to swimming a world record without any warm-up in training. At the time, Alex and his coach Gennadi Touretski were based at the Australian Institute of Sport and Alex's training feats tempted me to train with them at the AIS.

Ironically, I did learn to swim fast times regularly in training, not with Gennadi but with Scott and not in 1993 but in 1995 and onwards. Coincidentally, Scott followed the same mantra. He maintained you need to be able to produce your best regularly so then you yourself know you can swim fast whenever you want. As a spectator to Alex's training feats I never would have believed I could do the same, but the more practice I gained at swimming fast regularly the more it became a natural part of my psyche.

Before I moved to Scott, I rarely did maximum 200m butterfly efforts so when I got up to race them I was a bit scared and didn't have the confidence in my performance. Scott's training program was very daunting at first and for the first few weeks I couldn't do a whole week's work without dying. It took me a year to adjust to the program and I still haven't fully perfected it. I am continually challenged. But now I do maximum 200m butterfly efforts all the time and I no longer find them a big deal.

The hard work paid off in Atlanta. I was able to stand on the block and have the confidence to know I could swim fast whenever I wanted. Instead of dreaming about swimming fast, I had come to expect it. Nothing can boost your self-belief more than when you stand to face your toughest challenge and you know you can do it.

CHAPTER
FOCUS

- If you don't believe, you won't achieve. Hard work and determination will only get you so far.

- Never underestimate the importance of a happy and stimulating work environment.

- Comparison with others will often bring doubt about your own progress. Self-focus on what you have to do to achieve will increase your self-belief.

- Have the courage to break through the pain barrier and turn a negative into a positive.

- If you have only one goal in your life then it should be to improve. There is nothing better for building self-belief than knowing you have done something better than you have ever done it before.

- Analysing weaknesses and preparing thoroughly are your foundation stones in building self-belief and erasing self-doubt.

- Positive feedback is one of the best tools for building confidence and self-belief.

- Self-belief is knowing you can be successful when it counts. By regularly performing at your top level, what you once dreamt about achieving you come to expect.

PART THREE

Finishing strongly

1996

Every chapter in life has an ending, and after a tentative start and dramatic twist in the middle I was determined to bring about a happy ending in Atlanta. 1996 did not start well. Our pool was hijacked by the media juggernaut after Sam Riley tested positive to a headache tablet. Then I was sick on the eve of my race at the Olympic trials. The time leading up to Atlanta was the hardest I have worked to date. Some training sessions were so demanding and so tough I would crawl out of the pool in pain.

But without realising it, 1996 was an ideal preparation. The hardships only intensified my focus and vision of gold. The actual gold medal race felt easy compared with what I had been through in 1996.

Once on the blocks in Atlanta I was prepared for my toughest rivals and my fiercest test, which included racing against controversial Irish swimmer and three-time Olympic gold medallist Michelle Smith. I simply believed, focused and won the most important race of my life. This time I knew how to finish strongly and claim the most coveted prize in sport.

3

CHAPTER SEVEN

FOCUS

'No bird soars too high, who soars with his own wings.' **WILLIAM BLAKE**

'To be a winner, one must be totally committed. Total commitment means being willing to do whatever is necessary to become successful.' **FORREST GREGG**

E **lli Overton raised her arms in the air in triumph.** Only moments earlier another friend experienced the same sensation. The winning feeling of being on top of the world. But I couldn't join in their celebration. I was too embarrassed.

The squad was having fun after a tough training session and some of the swimmers were pretending how they would celebrate if they won at the Olympics. Elli's arms were pumped up and she looked so excited, but when it came to my turn I couldn't do it. I have never been good at showing my feelings and making a big deal of things and I couldn't raise my hands in the air, no matter how harmless it seemed. It just didn't come naturally to me, especially when I hadn't won yet. But there was more to it than that. I didn't want to tempt fate. If I pretended I had won it might somehow put a jinx on the gold medal and I wouldn't win. I didn't want to risk it.

I know this may sound intense but at the time the gold medal meant just about everything to me. Throughout my career I'd always aimed to do my best and had been content with international silver and bronze medals. But now, after 14 years of competitive swimming I was no longer happy with a silver or bronze medal. I didn't want anything to jeopardise an Olympic gold medal.

During the past couple of weeks of training I had never been so focused, maybe because the final piece in the puzzle which formed my self-belief had just been fitted. I was at an Australian squad butterfly camp at Singapore in June when head coach Don Talbot pulled me aside for a special talk. I knew I had been swimming well, because I always do my best in training when there is a lot of competition. I was competing against such swimmers as Michael Klim, Geoff Huegill, Greg Shaw, Angie Kennedy and Julia Ham. We did lots of quality sessions and I swam well, which really lifted my confidence. My training times indicated I was on track to swim well in Atlanta.

Don sometimes has private talks with swimmers. He called me in at the camp and said something like, 'Do you know you can be an absolute legend in Atlanta? You can come home with three Olympic gold medals.' He was talking about the 100m and 200m butterfly and the medley relay.

Suddenly I started to shake inside as Don's belief in me started to register. I finally allowed myself to get excited about my swimming potential. For years I had shut out any suggestion I could be an Olympic champion. In the past my self-doubts had attacked anything that could have become a foundation for my self-belief. Whenever someone said I could be a world-beater, my self-doubts immediately made me immune to the thought.

At this memorable meeting Don told me I didn't have enough confidence in my swimming. He told me I was a better swimmer than I thought I was and I could do better than what I was doing. Then he said, 'Don't you realise you can win a lot of medals in Atlanta?' Suddenly, with my self-doubts deflated, nothing was restricting my self-belief from growing. When Don told me I could win a gold medal at the Atlanta Olympics, I finally believed him. It registered that people had belief in me and I could soar as high as I wanted.

Don also said I could be a real legend like Shane Gould or Dawn Fraser. I had finally achieved self-belief but this suggestion was stretching it. He told me later he had deliberately used famous Australian female swimmers like Shane and Dawn so I could associate with their achievements. I think Don wanted me to develop an ego strong enough to show the world I was the best. That I had realised my potential and I had finally believed in myself.

The speech had such an effect on me because Don had never spoken to me like that before. I came back from the camp in Singapore with renewed fire and focus that I not only wanted to be the best but I knew I could be the best. But I kept this fire well hidden because I wanted my swimming to do my talking. Don's pep talk helped me to not only keep on striving to do my best but freed my wings from their cage of self-doubt. I knew I could soar to the heights of an Olympic gold medal.

A DRESS REHEARSAL FOR THE BIG EVENT

With every big event or challenge, whether it is sitting for an exam or speaking at a sales conference, it always helps to have a dress rehearsal. A dress rehearsal gives you the luxury of monitoring your progress and knowing whether you are on track for success. Dress rehearsals help you pick up key preparation faults, and if your dress rehearsal goes to plan then you know you have a formula that works. This can be a crucial confidence-builder for your big event.

The 1995 Pan Pac Championships were my dress rehearsal for the 1996 Olympic Games. They were held in the same city, in the same pool, and against similar competition as the Atlanta Olympics. Although one of the few differences between the Pan Pacs and the Olympics was that the Chinese were not competing.

In February the United States, Canada and Australia had voted on China being banned from the 1995 Pan Pac competition in August, because they believed the Chinese were guilty of institutionalised doping. The anti-drug campaign had stepped up in 1995 and FINA announced more stringent out-of-competition drug testing, which was progress. But enforcing a ban against China at the Pan Pacs was a real victory for the anti-drug campaign. Hopefully the ban would embarrass and shame the Chinese about their drug-using reputation and keep the pressure on them to stay clean.

I couldn't have hoped for a better dress rehearsal for my 200m butterfly at the 1995 Pan Pacs. The Pan Pacs are the only championships that hold the 200m butterfly on the first day, so they provide an ideal opportunity for me to swim a good time before I'm loaded down with my other events. I was under world record pace for the first 150 metres and swam a 2:07.29. I was the third fastest swimmer ever behind American Mary T. Meagher and China's Limin Liu. The American crowd was fantastic and gave me a standing ovation, which was an amazing feeling. Nothing could have given me more confidence for my Olympic campaign.

The only thing that didn't go to plan was that I was temporarily disqualified in the final of the 100m butterfly after an official alleged my shoulder had illegally dipped in my turns. But then the judge couldn't remember which shoulder had dipped so I was reinstated as the winner.

This ended up being a bonus because it alerted Scott and I to the fact that I occasionally dipped my shoulder in the turns. It was a bad habit that had snuck in during all the thousands of turns I did at training. To be disqualified, even temporarily, upset me and I actually knocked over three chairs when I went to the marshalling area to get my bag before I warmed down. What had really irked me was that when the big 'DQ' appeared against my name on the board, runner-up American swimmer Jenny Thompson jumped up and down shouting she had won.

Disqualification was not a pleasant experience but I realised it was better that it happened now and not at the Olympics. I came back from the Pan Pacs armed with the valuable information that I needed to improve my turns. Besides my turns I knew I had a successful formula. I had learnt from other swimmers' mistakes not to change things that worked. For example, Jenny Thompson went on a radical diet before the 1996 US Olympic trials which backfired because she lost much of her trademark strength and failed to make an individual event for Atlanta.

So I came back from the Pan Pacs with a clearer picture of where I stood leading to the Atlanta Olympics. I went to the championships hoping I would swim well and I left knowing I could swim well. I remember standing on the dais and hearing the Australian anthem and then saying to myself, I want to be standing here this time next year. I had tasted success and I wanted more.

My dress rehearsal not only gave me much needed confidence but I learnt valuable lessons about what I needed to change and what was working. I knew with another year of dedication and belief in my new program that anything was possible. My dream of winning an Olympic gold medal seemed a rung closer.

MAKING THE MOST OF POSITIVES

Don't be afraid if things start to go your way. Make the most of the positives to further build your confidence and self-belief. The key to success is knowing how to ride both the negatives and positives.

At the end of 1995 the situation with my swimming could not have been more positive. Internationally, the swimming officials finally seemed to be cracking down on China. Chinese swimmers had collected 19 positive drug tests over the past three years and this had finally sunk into FINA, which voted 26–13 on an Australian motion to double the ban for a positive drug test from two to four years at the FINA conference in November 1995. This was a major victory and a welcome sign leading up to the Atlanta Olympics.

On the national front I surprised everyone, including myself, when I was named the Australian Swimmer of the Year in November 1995. I had won three gold medals and two silver medals at the Pan Pacs and I had broken six Commonwealth records in the past 12 months under Scott. At the end of 1995 I was ranked world number one in the 100m butterfly and 200m butterfly and I was a member of Australia's 4 × 100m medley relay team, which also held the world's top ranking.

Then more positives came at the 1995 World Short Course Championships at Rio de Janeiro in Brazil when I gained another chance to race the Chinese. It was great to race my old adversary Limin Liu and I tasted my first victory against her in the 200m butterfly. The 1994 World Titles was the last time I had raced the Chinese and I saw them as my main rivals at the 1996 Olympics. Beating Limin in the 200m butterfly was a very important victory looking towards Atlanta. That triumph was an important stepping stone in my battle to gain self-belief in time for the 1996 Olympics.

All these positives in 1995 spurred me on to make greater sacrifices in my pursuit to win Olympic gold. My last big night where I allowed myself a few drinks was New Year's Eve. It's not hard to guess what I wished for on New Year's Eve.

I wanted to stand on the blocks in Atlanta and know I had done absolutely everything in my power to win gold. If I had drunk a couple of beers, then I would have known I had not done everything in my power and those beers would have come back to haunt me if I lost. Instead of sitting back and becoming complacent at the end of 1995 over all the positives, they gave me greater incentive and confidence as I focused on my goal of an Olympic gold medal.

THE ART OF VISUALISATION

Visualising became a key weapon in my campaign to win an Olympic gold medal. Constantly visualising my race helped me to overcome the pain in training and to keep a firm focus on my Olympic goal. It is amazing how powerful your mind is and how often when you visualise doing something, it happens how you imagined. From the start of 1996 and in the following intense build-up to Atlanta I realised that I had to be in the right mental frame of mind as well as doing the hard grind of training. So I constantly visualised my 200m butterfly race. The first tool I used to visualise my race was a photograph I had taken of the Atlanta Olympic pool at the 1995 Pan Pac Championships. I put the photo beside my bed so it gave me a reason to drag myself out of bed at 5 am. Whenever I felt low or didn't feel like going to training, I would just look at the photo of the venue of my goal and it gave me an incentive. The photo reminded me of my focus and commitment.

By the time the Olympics came around, after a year of viewing the photograph, I felt I knew every inch of the pool. I have found it helps to visualise achieving something in a familiar setting. Once you become familiar with your surroundings you are more comfortable so, instead of worrying about your environment, you can just focus on your challenge. When I arrived in Atlanta I was already familiar and comfortable with my setting so I could focus on my Olympic goal.

Leading to Atlanta the race would constantly go through my head. I could be anywhere and I would suddenly visualise it. I would be driving somewhere and the race would be in my head. Even once when I was in mass. Of course, when I visualised I would always win.

I remember I had a dream about my race one night a couple of months before the Olympics and I told Scott the next day. I dreamt I touched the wall and I couldn't see where I had come in the 200m butterfly but I turned around and saw I had done a 2:04.5, almost three seconds faster than my personal best. It also would have been a new world record. I remember thinking, Well I definitely must have won. But in the dream I couldn't see who was first or second.

Probably the biggest benefit from visualising was the ability to endure the pain in training. Instead of pain dominating my thoughts I had my Olympic race to keep me striving and going hard in training. I really needed a goal to visualise and focus on to get through the toughest sets, so whenever I started to hurt I would just picture my final lap in the 200m butterfly.

Whenever I visualised, I used my 1992 Olympic and 1994 World Championship races when I turned with others in the final lap but this time I would be the one pulling away and finishing strongly to be the first to touch the wall. Whenever I raced somebody or I was hurting in training I imagined I was on the last lap and it made me train faster and harder because I wanted to win.

ACHIEVING A WINNING FOCUS

You may have talent, determination and belief but nothing can replace a winning focus. A winning focus is when your resolution to win powers you to overcome any obstacle and distraction standing in the way of your goal. If you feel your focus weakening then look to your goal for motivation. Striving for a goal should be the driving force in a winning focus.

I first thought about the Atlanta Olympics straight after the Barcelona Olympics. After a bronze medal performance at my first Olympics it was only natural to think ahead to Atlanta and to aim a step higher. By 1996 the level of my focus moved to the highest gear. I was able to use my experience from Barcelona, when I got carried away with the excitement of going to the Olympics. This time I turned the focus on only my swimming.

Never in my life have I been so focused as I was in the months leading to Atlanta. I had a permanent burning drive for success and everything I did revolved around winning a gold medal. Anything I thought that would help me win a gold medal I did. I wouldn't even contemplate doing things if I didn't think they would help me win.

Consequently, in 1996, I didn't have much of a social life. In fact, I only went out socially or went out at night if I thought it would help me win a gold medal. When I needed to do extra training, I trained: if I needed more sleep, I slept. Rest and recovery became a major emphasis as the training became harder leading to Atlanta.

I saw training as my way of getting closer to an Olympic gold medal. Sometimes I couldn't wait to go to training to such an extent that I found it hard to sleep through the night. I was so excited about achieving my goal I couldn't be bothered to go through the sleeping process. I was striving at such a level of intensity and commitment, that it would have been impossible to be that driven permanently. Nothing could sway my focus because I wanted to be sure I had done everything I could to achieve my goal. I knew winning a gold medal would make all the sacrifices worthwhile.

But my focus was tested several times leading to the 1996 Olympics when I had to climb obstacles or was forced to detour around distractions. Tests are a bonus and not a burden because they give you practice at meeting your greatest challenge and in surviving them your confidence and focus increase. I learnt to put immediate obstacles into a long-term context and look ahead to the opportunities of tomorrow. Instead of weakening my resolve, the obstacles strengthened my focus and determination to win an Olympic gold medal.

Below are the tests I faced leading to Atlanta and how I learnt to use my focus to overcome them. The tests gave me that final edge of toughness I needed for my performance in Atlanta.

SURVIVING THE TESTS OF FOCUS

Drug controversy

We were in the first weeks of 1996 and our Olympic preparation was going quietly and smoothly until the story appeared in the media that Sam Riley had taken a headache tablet that contained a banned substance. Sam had suffered from a headache for more than a week on the eve of the World Short Course Championships in Rio de Janerio in Brazil in December 1995. She had tried massage, physiotherapy and icepacks but no treatment had brought relief – and about 11 o'clock one night she'd reached desperation point. Not wanting to wake up anybody Sam called Scott who had a headache tablet in his bag. I'd gone to the toilet and by the time I came out she'd taken it. It's unbelievable it happened because Sam is so careful about what medication she takes. She would not have questioned what Scott suggested.

Because Sam was a training partner and friend, I knew I would be on the periphery of the ensuing furore. I realised it would be a real test for my focus to not let it become a major distraction for my swimming. Reporters and news crews seemed to be camped permanently at our pool for a week and then the story continued to be major news for the months leading to Atlanta. At one stage it seemed likely Scott would be unable to attend the Olympics as he took the brunt of the punishment.

One of the hardest things about a winning focus was that to have the tunnel vision required to win in Atlanta meant I could not be there for Sam 100 per cent of the time. It was a hard time for Sam and Scott but they never stopped impressing me with their attitude. Sam showed a lot of inner strength. She always put on a brave front while she privately dealt with the crisis. Scott was amazing how he never showed signs of the strain in training. Away from the pool he was fighting hard to lessen the ban but at the pool it was training as normal and he remained the happy and positive coach he always has been.

I knew if my focus could survive this test it could survive anything. At the heart of my focus was my goal. At the time I felt it was my best chance, if not my only chance, to win an Olympic gold medal. At 23 years of age I was considered fairly old for a swimmer so I knew I couldn't afford to let anything stand in my way. My driving focus and determination to be the Olympic champion helped me to form blinkers so I could concentrate on what I had to do and not be distracted by anything else. When I turned up to training I was there to train and not to get involved in any other situation and away from training I never made Sam's crisis my business.

When it looked like Scott – the man who had been in the driving seat of getting me back on track mentally and physically for an Olympic gold medal – would not be on pool deck to support me for my moment of truth after all our hard work together, I had to search inside for that extra focus and strength to become a self-sufficient swimmer.

I realised I had come too far and had made too many sacrifices to let anything deter me now. I developed the mindset that nothing could stop me winning an Olympic gold medal, not even being without my coach in Atlanta. Just hours before the Australian team's departure Scott won his appeal and he was allowed at pool deck in Atlanta. But by that time I had already faced my test of focus and won.

Pressure-packed Olympic trials

Olympic trials are just about the worst competitions you can imagine because no team berth is more valued than for the Olympics. Then, to further test your nerves and focus, in the Olympic trials only two swimmers are allowed per event when most other competitions take three every event.

Trials are worse than the actual competition because there you just have to swim your best while at the trials often swimming your best is not good enough. Your first and only priority is to qualify for the Australian team. And then it's easy to fall into the trap of letting the behind-the-scenes dramas distract your focus and performance. The 1996 Olympic trials were my third so I had gained a lot of experience at handling the distractions but, as it turned out, these Olympic trials were the toughest I had ever faced.

The trials attracted much more media coverage than they normally did and suddenly, with swimmers such as Sam and Kieren Perkins struggling, there was a great deal of pressure on all the experienced swimmers to perform. So, if you let your focus be distracted by the pressure it was easy to be swept up by it. My focus wavered slightly and I started to feel a bit of pressure. I was confident I would make the team but I wanted to make sure I made it in all the events I set out to do. I achieved this but my swims were not spectacular.

Then I got sick before my 200m butterfly but I knew I had to swim if I wanted to make the team. I didn't want to leave anything to chance and rely on selectors. In the warm-up I was throwing up after every lap. It was the worst I have ever felt before a race but somehow I managed to win.

The trials ended up being an ideal dress rehearsal for the focus required at Atlanta. Almost the identical happened there when many of the top guns didn't do as well as expected. But by Atlanta my focus was rock-solid. I learnt from the trials I should never let the media hype and pressure weaken my focus or my resolve.

Painful preparation

The pool sessions in the months before the 1996 Olympics were nothing like I had experienced before. Some days were so tough I think I would have hopped out of the pool if Scott hadn't been there. In fact, during those sessions I constantly thought about retiring after the 1996 Olympics. The thought of never having to push myself through the pain barrier again in another training set was very appealing. I kept thinking to myself, I can't forget what this training is like and how much I'm hurting. It's important to remember the price you have paid for success.

If I did have a downer Scott knew how to motivate me. Sometimes he made me angry in heart rate sets to make me go faster. He'd say things like, 'Oh fine, if you don't want to do your best, take the easy option or the soft option' or 'We'll just win the bronze medal again, if that's how you want to train'. I didn't need too much help in regaining my focus leading to Atlanta, but now and then I needed extra motivation.

One reason we pushed so hard in training was so the actual race wouldn't seem as painful. Throughout my career I had always breathed between each stroke but with Scott I started to breathe between every two strokes for training sets. I then learnt to breathe every three strokes for the last 25 metres in each training distance and this really hurt!

I've always hated holding my breath under water and several times in training leading to Atlanta the panicky feeling returned and I couldn't breathe when I had pushed myself to the edge. It was the same panicky feeling that prevented me from reaching the other side of the pool when I was younger. But now my self-belief and focus was a lot stronger and the feeling didn't stop me from striving for my goal.

After the trials Scott started to count down the days until our departure for Atlanta. Fortunately it was only a short preparation of about 12 weeks, and counting down was another way of overcoming the tough training. After every session we could say there was one less hard session of training left, which helped make the goal seem closer.

Steered by a consistent driving force, an Olympic gold medal, my training was never so consistent and effective. By the time I had left for Atlanta I had gained a winning focus that could overcome any training hardships or powerful distractions.

CHAPTER
FOCUS

- Dress rehearsals help you to pick up key preparation faults and the strengths of your formula, which is a crucial confidence-builder for your big event.

- The key to success is knowing how to ride both the negatives and positives. Positives shouldn't promote complacency but instead provide further incentives to achieving your goal.

- Visualising your challenge helps to strengthen your focus and, more often than not, what you visualise you will achieve.

- You may have talent, determination and belief but nothing can replace a winning focus, when your resolution to win powers you to overcome any obstacle and distraction standing in the way of your goal.

- If you do feel your focus weakening then look to your goal for motivation. Striving for a goal should always be the driving force in a winning focus.

- Tests are a bonus because they not only give you practice at meeting your greatest challenge but in surviving them, your confidence, determination and focus are increased.

CHAPTER EIGHT

DELIVERING

'A champion is not a special person but a person who does special things.' **UNKNOWN**

'Everybody has the same amount of energy. But most people waste it in a thousand different ways. I channel all mine into a single positive direction and sacrifice everything to it.' **PABLO PICASSO**

There **was no turning back.** I was on the plane for Atlanta and in less than three weeks I would know the answer to my four-year Olympic quest.

I usually get a really sick, nervous feeling when I step on a plane for a competition, and I say to myself, 'Well, I can only do my best and then hope that's good enough to win'. But the Atlanta Olympics were special. As with all competitions I couldn't wait until the Olympics were over, but this time I didn't have the usual pre-competition sinking feeling. Boarding the plane, I still felt nervous but the nerves were accompanied by excitement and not doubt. After all the hard work, training and sacrifices I was looking forward to racing. At last I possessed that serene confidence that comes from knowing I had done everything I could in training and preparation.

It has always helped me to count down to a major event. This time, once I was on the plane I had only 18 days until the Olympic competition started in Atlanta. Then you count down until it's the day of the race when you wake up and think, Well I only have 12 hours to go and this will all be over. Then by the time I leave my room for the finals I think, Next time I walk back into this room I could be a gold medallist. It's sort of weird when you think of things in that way.

Swimming and competing are like most things: you enjoy some aspects but you don't enjoy others. When I'm sitting in the marshalling area it's always, 'What do I do this for?' and 'I don't want to be here'. For the 10 minutes before the race I question why I continue to swim because the tension can be unbelievable. But then after a race I get the biggest buzz and I feel on a high.

The Olympics promised an even bigger buzz than normal after a pact I'd made with Sam Riley: if I won a gold medal I would go bungy jumping and if Sam won a gold medal she would do a parachute jump. I suppose I was desperate to win a gold medal and so I agreed to any crazy scheme, like bungy jumping. A couple of years before they were giving away free bungy jumps and Sam readily had a go but I couldn't bring myself to jump. It looked like a bungy jump was going to be the price I paid to achieve my dream of a gold medal.

KEEPING FOCUS IN A DIFFICULT ENVIRONMENT

Like your form, your focus has to also peak for major challenges which is why practice in training and lead-up events is so important. Very few competitions or events offer easy environments but you always have to rise above any distractions or changes of plan with a solid self-focus. Those with concrete focuses will be the ones who triumph.

The three weeks leading to the Olympic competition was probably the most difficult competition lead-up in my eight years in the Australian team. The first few days were ideal as the Australian swimming team was based at Athens, a university town 104 kilometres north-east of Atlanta. We had stayed in Athens before the Pan Pacific Championships in 1995 when Australia had one of its best competitions in history. It would have been great to have another long stay but it was not to be because ACOG (the Atlanta Organising Committee) decided they needed the University of Georgia campus. ACOG needed two weeks to set up a day village for rhythmic gymnastics, volleyball and soccer.

Don Talbot had originally wanted the facility until 15 July, when we would then move our base to Atlanta. Instead we were kicked out on 7 July, 14 days before the competition started. So the Australians were one of the first teams to arrive at the massive Olympic village, located at the Georgia Institute of Technology. The village is like a town for athletes with food, administration and medical centres. Fortunately the village and dining hall were conveniently located next door to the pool, which meant the pool was in walking distance or a short tram ride away.

When you arrive at a competition site, especially the

Olympics, you cannot help but get excited and nervous. It's a weird feeling to finally arrive at the place you have dreamt about triumphing at for so long. Suddenly you realise your moment of truth is so close. But then we had a two-week wait and many of the swimmers found it difficult to maintain their competition excitement and focus.

Probably the biggest problem for a lot of the athletes was boredom. We filled in time with great difficulty. There wasn't much to do in the village and it felt like we were marking time. Sam and I hung around friends and stretched our times in the food hall as much as possible. One day the Australian team visited the tourist attraction Stone Mountain. But we weren't meant to walk around too much or do too much activity so we didn't waste energy for the competition. After so many years in the Australian team I've learnt to be careful about conserving my energy. When I first made an Olympic team in 1992 there were many distractions. You could get caught up in playing the games, running around the village and eating all the junk food.

So I've just learnt how to be very focused and things I did in Barcelona, I would never have done in Atlanta. At Barcelona with four days before the swimming started, Sam and I decided to go on a bike ride. We caught a train into town, bought a bicycle each and rode back to the village through the traffic. And we got lost. We cycled for ages and it was boiling hot. It was not the best activity for conserving energy. To top it off I hurt my knee riding down some stairs. No way was I going to risk my health and do something stupid like that again.

In Atlanta we usually trained the same time we were going to race so we trained and stretched in the morning at about 9 o'clock. We were training in the pool twice a day but it wasn't hard training, just tapering. At first the training was great because the village wasn't crowded and we had almost a free rein in the pool. But once the village started to fill-up we had interrupted training. We had to share the pool and it was becoming very squashy.

It was a tough training environment but I learnt to focus on what I needed to do and not worry about the crowded lanes and other distractions. The magic of the Atlanta pool and the environment had certainly faded for many of the Australian swimmers by the end of our fortnight stay, before competition had even started.

I remember one funny incident that helped relieve the monotony of that fortnight. Our rooms were set up just how you would expect of a university dormitory: two people to a room with the toilets down the end of the corridor. Each room had power points that went through to the other side so, consequently, you could hear straight through to the other room.

Sam and I were sitting in our room one night and I don't know how we discovered it, but we found we could hear what our neighbours Nicole Stevensen and Hayley Lewis were talking about next door. So every night when we went to bed, for entertainment we would put our ears to the power points and listen to what they were saying. Unbeknownst to us, Nicole and Hayley had discovered this little trick before us and could hear what we were saying.

One night all four of us were sitting there with our ears against the power points waiting for someone to talk. Nicole started with some really gossipy thing that she thought would get us talking. By then we realised they too were listening, so we started saying stuff like: 'Oh Nicole, she's got such beautiful eyes, those lashes really enhance her eyes, they make her look beautiful.' And we were making up stories about how Sam got engaged and congratulating her and how I was planning to have a couple of babies before the year 2000. Soon everyone was laughing and Nicole and Hayley came into our room. It was about 1 am and we were laughing so hard tears were coming down. It woke a few people up and the manager told us to be quiet but I really needed that laugh after the days of boredom.

In the nervous and tense wait before events there's a fine line between keeping your focus on why you are there and over-focusing. You have to lock out any distractions but at the same time it's unhealthy to sit in your room when you cannot help but think about the race. Whenever I could feel myself over-analysing I always sought the company of other swimmers or my coach. I realised it was important I didn't spend too much time dwelling on the race and picking on any little point that could breed doubt. Over-focusing can be dangerous because it can be very draining on your energy. It's good to have a mix of relaxation and focus.

The change from Athens to the lengthy stay in Atlanta threw a lot of the swimmers in the lead-up to the Olympics. It is important not to panic when there is a change to a well-rehearsed procedure, especially before a major event. Experience has taught me to be self-sufficient and to look within myself for my strength and focus.

There was nothing I could do about arriving early in Atlanta and I had to make the best of a difficult situation. I believe the people who handled the difficult situation and kept their focus were the ones who swam the best in Atlanta. I recognised the situation was out of my hands and I had to ride the change and keep calm. Most importantly, I had to keep my focus on why I was in Atlanta – to win gold in the 200m butterfly.

Whatever hardship is thrown at you, you have to learn to be self-sufficient. Even though everyone faced the same problems of boredom and distraction, the key was to look forward to the competition. I never let my hunger for victory fade. My drive, focus and hunger for a gold medal was still as strong at the village as it was in the months leading to Atlanta.

THE IMPORTANCE OF TEAM SPIRIT

Team spirit will not guarantee victory but it can dramatically lift your chances for success. A team spirit surrounds a group of people with positive energy which creates a confident, focused and united platform to achieving success. Without a team spirit it comes back to the individual and how self-sufficient they are in building their own focus and self-belief.

Athens, our first destination for four days, was a great place to build team spirit. In Athens the team trained together, ate together and had a lot of fun together. Athens had such a good atmosphere with shops and restaurants just a short walk down-town. The team was close in Athens because it was such a small town. The pool was much better for training because we didn't have to share with a lot of countries like we did with Atlanta's crowded pool.

Once the team moved to the Atlanta village some of that togetherness was lost. The swimming team was housed on two levels of the university and because everyone had their differ-ent routines it was difficult to see the other swimmers regularly. We all stayed in our separate squads. A lot of people said Scott's squad was a separate team from everyone else. It's just that we had a lot of people in our squad and we are all good friends so we always hung around together.

Another situation that dampened the team spirit was the dis-integration of the rookie nights, when people who are new in the Australian swimming team have to do a skit or some other embarrassing deed in front of the rest of the team. Rookie nights help bring the team together and are always good fun.

In Atlanta the setting was the dining hall, where there was probably a thousand people, and the rookies had to dress up in their togs, caps and goggles and walk through and order their meal. Another group dressed up in outfits and make-up for a version of 'I Love the Night Life' from the movie *The Adventures of Priscilla, Queen of the Desert,* which they performed in McDonald's.

Rookies often poke fun at the older members of the team, but it's always been in a good spirit. Then, in 1995, the rookies paid out on heaps of the other swimmers and there was a lot of disharmony. They were really cruel to people. So in Atlanta the rookies were given a theme and the night was still fun, but it didn't have the same spontaneity as in the past, which probably hurt the team spirit.

In fact for me the Atlanta trip was probably the most un-humorous trip I've ever had with the Australian team. In Atlanta we were going through a transition stage which again made it difficult for a healthy team spirit to grow. Many of Australia's leaders had retired. Team leaders are mostly the older swimmers and it's usually members that aren't swimming that day. Conse-quently, I have never been a team leader because I usually swim every day.

In Atlanta there was no Andrew Baildon, Rod Lawson or Angus Waddell to rev up the team spirit. Many of the older ones in the team are like myself, not really team leaders. Nicole Stevensen was pretty good. Daniel Kowalski has a really good team spirit and often is in the stands cheering on friends, which is great considering his own heavy program. Kieren Perkins kept to himself pretty well in Atlanta. He was probably like me, just focusing mainly on his race.

Another method the Australians used for building the team spirit was starting competition days and the finals sessions with a team meeting. In the morning meeting they usually say how everyone has gone the night before and everyone claps. Then they say who is swimming today in what events and if they call your name, you stand up. Then everyone claps and there's another big cheer. The same procedure is used before the finals and there is a massive cheer for those in final A or B. It's quite funny how when we swim well, the media usually write how we have an excellent team spirit and then when we are not swimming well, they write we have a bad team spirit. In Atlanta it was true that our team spirit was down and everyone was a bit low after the swimming started. The team meetings were not doing their job.

Most team meetings are great fun and really lift you but in Atlanta they were having the opposite effect. A strong team spirit could have repelled the negative vibes that were allowed to breed in the Australian camp. The Australian team was not living up to expectations and negativity had seeped into the meetings.

Don may not be super-popular but I think he is a very good head coach and I don't think there is anyone else, at the moment, who could do the job he does. He does get some strange ideas for motivation, however. Don told us at one team meeting that the journalists were sharpening their pencils and they would write bad stories if we didn't swim well. This was just before we went into the finals, which I really don't think was the best motivation for us to swim well. I didn't feel any extra pressure but I'm sure what Don said would have created more pressure and expectation for other swimmers. It was certainly not something that lifted the team spirit.

Don brought the negative publicity into the team, when he could have ignored it and shielded us. Obviously people were feeling the heat in Atlanta. Most of the team seemed to be talking about the disappointing results and were getting down about it. Maybe Don should have told us to just concentrate on our swimming and not to worry about what's going on around us.

Finally it was left to the swimmers to try to rebuild the team spirit and Nicole Stevensen and Chris Fydler held an athletes only meeting midweek in Atlanta. Nicole and Chris brought it back to basics and really helped the team get back together. Everyone had been starting to dread going to team meetings. The team began to regain some team spirit with the relays when we won a silver and two bronze medals in the final days of the Atlanta competition. But by then it was almost too late.

There is no doubt team spirit is an important ingredient to success. The American swimming team was an example. The

Americans were all based in camp at Nashville, Tennessee. They didn't move to Atlanta until just before the competition started. This strategy enabled them to build a strong team atmosphere and I have no doubt this was one of the reasons for their successful campaign.

With a strong team spirit a group can feed on each other's positive energy which creates a confident, focused and exciting atmosphere that helps people achieve success. For most of the Atlanta Olympics the Australian swimmers lacked a team spirit and the unsettling forces of negativity, uncertainty and doubt were allowed to develop. It was left to the individual to be self-sufficient in building a winning focus and attitude. Fortunately I had gained a lot of practice in the past two years in developing a self-focus and self-belief to win an Olympic gold medal and didn't need to rely on team spirit.

WORDS WITH INSPIRATIONAL GREATS

Three people associated with Olympic gold medal performances all helped me in the two weeks leading to Atlanta. I met 1988 400m hurdles Olympic gold medallist Debbie Flintoff-King at lunch. We didn't talk much about the Olympics and my races but it was really good to have her around because she was just so normal. It made me realise normal, everyday-type people can become Olympic champions and achieve great things. I had always thought Olympic gold medallists were superhuman, but Debbie didn't have a big aura about her. She was a really down-to-earth person who had achieved something special.

Australia's best known swimming legend Dawn Fraser was also inspirational. Dawn talked to the 4 × 100m relay one lunchtime and she was great. She is really passionate about sport and Australia, but she is also pretty relaxed and down to earth. I have a lot of respect for what she has to say. She made winning a gold medal sound really easy. She mainly talked about her individual races and how she would walk out and say, 'Well, I'm the best here and the other competitors have to beat me'. She said otherwise you are thinking, Oh gosh, I've got to beat that person and that one. Her message was the other competitors had to beat you to win the race. She made it sound so simple that I left thinking, Well, I'm going to win this gold medal. When I walked out for the 200m butterfly final, I thought, Well the other competitors will have to swim bloody fast to beat me. And if they do, well good on them.

Dawn also said it was important to have a good team spirit and to give your best to your country. I believe Australians need that sort of encouragement because a lot of times at internationals, especially when you first start making swimming teams, Australians never think they are good enough to beat the Americans or Europeans. Many Australians have an inferiority complex, and I know it took me a long time to realise I could match the overseas competitors. You would fall into the trap of thinking they must be training more and have more advanced technology, but everyone starts on equal ground with two arms and two legs.

Another person who always has something motivational to say is Laurie Lawrence, who coached Olympic gold medallists Duncan Armstrong and Jon Sieben. The spooky thing is just before the Olympic Games started Laurie took a picture of myself and beach volleyball player Natalie Cook with past gold medallists John Devitt and Michael Wenden. When he was taking the photo he said, 'This one is of gold medallists'. It was weird, as though he knew I would win gold. Natalie, as an outside medal chance, won a bronze medal with Kerry Pottharst. It was encouraging Laurie had such faith in me, but at the time I didn't want him to put a jinx on the race. Looking back, it might be something I should try in future competitions.

For some reason Laurie has had great faith in me for a long time. I was a member of a target squad when I was 14 years old and Laurie singled me out and said I would do great things one day. I nervously giggled and he told me not to laugh because he was serious. Laurie always said I would win the gold medal in the 200m butterfly.

We did a lot of motivational team things with Laurie. We used to have singing sessions out in the quadrangle, in the middle of the accommodation in the Olympic village. We came out with songs like 'Give Me a Home Among the Gum Trees' and 'Waltzing Matilda' and then one day one of the track and field competitors brought out a guitar and started playing 'Tainted Love', which was rather good. Poor Laurie, the chorus to 'Tainted Love', was sung so much louder than for 'Waltzing Matilda', but it was still good to sing Australian songs.

AVOID TALKING REWARDS

Talking about and listening to discussions about rewards before your event is an unnecessary distraction. It builds expectation and sidetracks you from the focus of your challenge. A strong focus is the only way to repel such distractions and to make sure the reward becomes reality and doesn't stay a dream.

The Australian team carried high expectations coming into Atlanta, especially after outstanding performances at the 1995 Pan Pacific Championships and the World Short Course Titles. In contrast, the Americans had seemed to under-perform in both meets. Furthermore, Australia had seemed tantalisingly close to the Americans in the competitions of the past four years. We were encouraged after the Americans beat us by only one gold medal to claim the best nation title at the 1995 Pan Pac Championships.

Many people had written off the United States leading to the Atlanta Olympics and the American swimmers and coaches went along with it. The Americans downplayed the team's chances while they talked up the Chinese and Australian teams.

The Americans had learnt from the 1992 Olympics when they predicted success in the press and then failed to reach public expectation. This time, instead of the Americans talking medals, they won them. They finished as the leading nation with 26 medals including 13 gold.

In contrast, the Australian team was swamped by medal hype and expectation from the start and Don Talbot seemed to reinforce it. I remember going to one press conference before the Olympics started and Don was saying ours was the best team we had ever had and that we are going to win more medals than we have ever won before. He said it was 'the best racing Olympics in memory' because it was the most wide-open Olympics he could recall. Don said we would win more medals than we won in Barcelona (one gold, two silver and five bronze) as part of our aim to be the world's best swimming nation for the 2000 Olympics.

Australia's phenomenal success at the Commonwealth Games two years before also added to the expectation. Everyone swam off their tree and we won nearly every event but the Commonwealth Games are a different level of competition. The Olympics is undoubtedly the hardest competition to succeed at.

The talk about medals and the expectations were hard for the team to carry, especially when the weight fell on the shoulders of a handful of swimmers. At press conferences the main attention was on Sam and Kieren, who entered the Olympics as dual world champions. There was a lot of hype about Sam and the drug incident. Eighteen-year-old Michael Klim, who was ranked number one in the world in the 200m freestyle, also carried pressure and received a lot of coverage.

The medal talk continued during the Olympics, especially when Australia failed to meet medal expectations. For some of the Australian swimmers the talk about the medals became a distraction. Obviously every swimmer wants to win a medal and I suppose that's why it became such a talked-about subject.

Additionally, no one cares about fourth or they don't seem to. Matt Dunn finished fourth twice and fifth once. His efforts included two excellent individual swims but he didn't win a medal and then people who swim relay heats get a medal. While we need people to swim relay heats someone like Matt should get recognition even though he didn't get a medal. He deserved one.

I learnt not to let myself get caught up in the medal hype. Instead, Scott Volkers and I took a different approach. We took the underdog mentality in private and public. I hardly received any media attention, and never encouraged it, so I was left alone to focus on my race. Scott even spoke to some of the journalists asking them not to write too much about me. He tried to control the media pressure on me as much as he could. I never talked about medals or expectations and never read any newspapers so I could keep my focus on my task. I just got down to the basics and just focused on my swimming and not the rewards. I didn't want to talk about medals, I wanted to win them. I knew if I did everything right in my race, the rewards would come.

IGNORING OUTSIDE INFLUENCES

A key to delivering your best performance in an event such as an exam or an important work project is to ignore outside influences. If your workmates or friends are struggling you must not let it stop you from doing your best. Self-belief and self-focus will help you ignore any outside criticism or distraction.

Team performances

The Australian swimming team was struggling. Very few members produced personal bests and despite a healthy collection of bronze and silver medals, many of Australia's best known swimmers were disappointed in their efforts.

From day one when promising teenager Michael Klim was one of the favourites in the 200m freestyle and misjudged his heat and missed the final, Australia's fortunes didn't reach the level of expectation. Daniel Kowalski achieved an impressive haul of a silver (1500m) and two bronze (200m and 400m freestyle) medals, but I believe he was dissatisfied with his performance.

Nicole Stevensen missed the final for her favourite event, the 200m backstroke, and finished seventh in the 100m backstroke. Hayley Lewis and Stacey Gartrell missed the 800m final as strong medal contenders.

There were some outstanding efforts, such as Sarah Ryan who swam a personal best and finished sixth in the 100m freestyle final. Australia's youngest swimmer, Emma Johnson, at 16, put in a strong 400m individual medley performance, finishing fifth at 4:44.02. Scott Miller and Scott Goodman won silver and bronze in the 100m and 200m butterfly finals.

Closer to home, I could feel the disappointment and see the tears when friends and training partners Sam Riley and Elli Overton didn't meet their expectations. Sam won bronze in the 100m breaststroke and was fourth in the 200m breaststroke. Elli was a realistic medal chance but was disappointed to finish fifth in the 200m individual medley (2:16.04). It is difficult as roommates when one is doing really well and the other is not. I knew the feeling in 1994 when Sam won the 100m and 200m breaststroke at the World Championships and the Commonwealth Games. When I was feeling down I didn't want to spoil Sam's swimming high.

In Atlanta when Sam finished her events she stayed out of the room and often was with her boyfriend, now fiancé, Johann Koss. It was a very upsetting competition for Sam and I understood her need for private solace and she understood my need for a positive preparation without any distractions. I could've let the team's and especially my friends' swimming lows affect my performance. I knew how hard my friends had trained. We had trained side by side and I think both Elli and Sam deserved to be Olympic champions. More importantly, we had the same coach, we trained under the same methods and worked with the same taper. With an almost identical preparation I could be forgiven for thinking whatever went wrong with their performance could also affect me.

Instead, Scott kept my focus really positive. He made me believe Elli's and Sam's form had no bearing on my own. I realised I was the only person who had control over my swimming and I was able to keep my focus channelled on my performances alone.

Critics

The Australian swimming team couldn't escape from hearing the criticisms which remained for the whole week of competition. I deliberately didn't read any newspapers and Mum and Dad never told me about the media coverage in Australia. The first I heard about the press was from Don or from other swimmers who had spoken to their parents. I heard later Don had called the Australian swimmers 'cocky and careless'. It surprised me but Don has a psychology degree so maybe it was a way of motivating us.

Criticism, especially of Don, came from former swimming greats such as Steve Holland, Murray Rose, Jon Sieben, Queensland swimming officials and even the Australian Olympic Committee chairman John Coates. Mr Coates said the Australian public was entitled to be disappointed at the performance of the Olympic swimmers. He said the public funded the sporting programs and had been led to believe the swimming team would perform considerably better than it had.

It was especially upsetting when Neil Brookes and Duncan Armstrong started to criticise the swimming team on television. Apparently they said our turns and starts were too slow and we were being left behind in the relay changeovers. They said we needed to be more aggressive. A lot of the team were disappointed because Neil and Duncan are one of us, swimmers. They have won Olympic gold medals and they know what the pressure is like. It was like one of our own bagging us.

I never allowed myself to get swept up by the criticisms. To be honest, I was so close to achieving my goal and so focused on my 200m butterfly race that I didn't care what anyone else thought. You can't worry about the drama going on around you. You have to concentrate on yourself. You also have to remember a lot of the drama is fleeting and at the end of the day the only thing everyone remembers is who has won the Olympic gold medals.

ACHIEVING YOUR COMPETITION FOCUS

It is important to be focused throughout your campaign for success but no time is more vital than the minutes leading to your event. It is very hard to triumph without being in the right frame of mind and without being focused.

By the Atlanta Olympics I had made every Australian team for the past eight years, but despite the experience I still made mistakes. One of them was with my race focus. I found it hard to get excited for some of my events. I was so focused on my 200m butterfly that I struggled with my focus for the 200m freestyle and 100m butterfly. For the 200m freestyle Scott talked to me about what it meant to be swimming the event in the Olympic Games. It was pretty obvious motivational stuff but sometimes you really need to hear it to regain the excitement.

I had taken the pressure off myself so much because I thought I had no chance of winning the event that I didn't get nervous. I would get more nervous for the 200m freestyle at the State Titles where I'm expected to win or I expect myself to win. In Atlanta I expected to make the final but I had to hear from my coach that I could win a medal in the event and I was not far from the top seeds. The motivational talk paid off. I finished fifth and swam a personal best, 1:59.87, and became the first Australian woman since Michelle Pearson in the 1984 Olympics to swim under two minutes (1.59.79) for the 200m freestyle. I missed a bronze medal by .31 of a second.

My main problem for the 100m butterfly was a lack of self-focus and self-belief. I saw the 100m butterfly as a fill-in race for the 200m butterfly and had talked myself out of having any chance to win a medal. I am kicking myself now because the race was won by American Amy Van Dyken in a relatively slow time (59.13), ahead of my old Chinese rival Limin Liu (59.14). The world record is 57.93. I finished fifth with the disappointing time (1:00.17), which was below my best (59.58). This was the event I won a bronze medal in at the 1994 World Championships behind two Chinese who were believed to be on drugs.

Fortunately I gained the right focus to produce strong swims in the 4 × 100m medley relay, which won the silver medal, and in the 4 × 200m freestyle relay, which won bronze.

THE IMPORTANCE OF SLEEP

Sleep is one of the most important aspects of any challenge. Everyone needs to be refreshed and ready to perform. Sleep most often comes when you are relaxed and confident. Lying in bed at night is when you are often swamped by problems and doubts. That is why relaxation and confidence are so important.

I had really wanted to go to the Atlanta Opening Ceremony, especially when there was a strong chance it could be my last Olympics. It was a huge sacrifice not to go but I was swimming in two days' time and the ceremony is very tiring and draining. You sit or stand around for hours and hours and the Australian team didn't get back until 2 o'clock the next morning. And then with all the excitement it's difficult to get to sleep. I rated my sleep more important than the opening ceremony, no matter how large a sacrifice.

In fact, I treasure my sleep so much I have never been to an opening ceremony, never mind watching a full opening ceremony. I had to be rested and refreshed for my biggest ever challenge. Unfortunately I've never been a good sleeper during competitions. Ever since I realised the enormity of representing Australia, at the 1990 Commonwealth trials, I have suffered from nerves and have found it difficult to sleep. And one of the things I've learnt is not to get carried away with what's happening around me, like the opening ceremony, because otherwise it can be even more difficult to settle down and sleep.

The Americans rated sleep so highly, one of the American swimmers was telling me to help them with their sleep the whole team took Melatonin, some magic jet-lag drug that is banned in Australia.

It's when I'm trying to get to sleep many of my problems and doubts surface, and Atlanta was no different. I remember getting a lot of confidence from the 200m freestyle swim because I felt I was swimming the best I had ever swum. But two nights later the sleeping blues hit me again when I went to bed with a lot of doubts after my 100m butterfly race, when I finished fifth in a slow time. After such an encouraging start to Atlanta I started to wonder if maybe I was not swimming well, or my taper was out or maybe I was in a trough. The race felt really stiff and forced and maybe if I had been more relaxed the result could have been different. You cannot help but analyse after a bad race, especially when you are trying to get to sleep. The way I overcame my doubts and then got some sleep was to find my self-belief. I realised every race was different and I made myself believe the 100m butterfly result could have no bearing on my main event.

Throughout Atlanta I had heaps of trouble sleeping the night before my races. If I started to think about the 200m butterfly, I couldn't sleep at all. The night before the 200m butterfly was the hardest night to get to sleep. I was still awake at 2 am because I was excited. After so many months and then days of counting down suddenly the night before had arrived. I could imagine myself swimming really well and I just wanted to get out to the pool and swim. I was lying there, reading my book and listening to my Walkman. I was mainly thinking about my race. I imagined what I would be thinking behind the block, that I had trained four years for this moment and it better work out. I used my self-belief to turn my doubts into positive thoughts. I knew the first three laps would be pretty good, they always are in my 200m butterfly. I knew it would come down to the final lap. Whenever I imagined the race it was always close for three laps and then I knew I had to pull away on the last lap. I always visualised myself finishing strongly.

I woke up at 6 am with big dark rings under my eyes. I felt all right because I was running on adrenalin. Not surprisingly, I spent most of the second week of Atlanta catching up on sleep.

Countdown – only 13 hours and 33 minutes.

CHAPTER
FOCUS

- It's important when there are distractions or a sudden change of plan not to panic but instead to look within for strength and self-focus to make the best out of a difficult situation.

- Team spirit increases the chances of success because a group is surrounded by positive energy which creates a confident and focused atmosphere.

- Talking about the rewards before the event builds expectation and then sidetracks you from the focus of your challenge, so instead of the reward becoming a reality, it stays a dream.

- A self-belief and self-focus will help you ignore any outside criticism or distraction.

- It's important to be focused throughout your campaign for success but no time is more vital than the minutes leading to your event. It's very hard to triumph if you're not in the right frame of mind.

- Sleep is one of the most important aspects of any challenge. You need to be confident and relaxed to repel the self-doubts which come in the night, and to sleep.

CHAPTER NINE

GOLD

'One of the greatest pleasures in life is achieving things that people say can't be done.' **SCOTT VOLKERS**

'You never worry about outside pressure. The pressure of satisfying yourself by being number one is the only one that counts.'
JOHN RALSTON

A lot of people have asked me if I felt increased pressure in my 200m butterfly final because Australia had not yet won a swimming gold medal after six days of racing. I felt less pressure. When the swimming team is winning gold medals left, right and centre you really feel like you have to win to be part of it. That can be pressure. But when no Australian swimmer has won a gold medal, winning becomes a big challenge.

Here we were on the last day of competition in Atlanta and I could become the first in the Australian swimming team to win a gold medal. Australia had won two silver and five bronze medals in the pool. Instead of the challenge being a burden, I was lifted by it.

There had been times in the past few years when I felt my heavy workload for Australia in competitions had been for nothing. I felt I struggled for recognition and I was sometimes a forgotten member of the swim team. I have never been a headline grabber but just trained 10 times a week and quietly went about my business. I suppose the media didn't see my life as exciting. There was nothing sensational to report on, just that I could sometimes swim fast.

The lack of publicity was something that didn't worry me too much since publicity wasn't my reason for swimming. But I had used this lack as a huge motivator in 1996. I felt no one cared about my swimming, which made me more determined. Actions speak louder than words. I thought, I'll show them. Just watch what I can do. Suddenly here was my chance to do something special.

I felt for the swimmers who had been disappointed in their results, but this was a moment I had been waiting so long for. It was an ideal build-up for my race. Forget about the pressure. I was ready for the gold.

My focus was so strong for the 200m butterfly it was all I could think about 24 hours beforehand, even when I was standing on the podium after winning a bronze medal as a member of the 4 x 200m freestyle relay. People said I looked distracted and disinterested on the podium, like I didn't want to be there. And it was true. All I could think was, I hope I'm standing on this podium in 24 hours' time with a gold medal around my neck. I couldn't wait to get off the podium, do my swim down and get back to my room to prepare for my 200m butterfly. Then the media wanted photographs and I was getting a bit annoyed. It was great to win a bronze medal but I wanted to go so I could be ready for my main event.

Every day Scott would remind me I had two focuses at this meet: each event every day and then the 200m butterfly at the end of the week. It was good to have the other events because they kept me race-fit and focused on competing as I headed towards my Olympic mission. The relays had especially given me a lift after winning silver and bronze medals, but really I had come to Atlanta for the gold medal in the 200m butterfly.

I had survived my career low and found the courage to face my crossroad. I had worked hard to achieve the self-belief and self-focus to be ready for my greatest challenge. Then I had waited all week in Atlanta because I knew only the 200m butterfly could provide my moment of truth.

During the week Scott had been making up inspiring sayings on his computer and then sticking them on everyone's doors. It was a great idea and it helped to motivate everybody. For my 200m butterfly race he got another brainwave. Just after my heat he gave me a piece of paper. It was the saying from his door: 'One of the greatest pleasures in life is achieving things that people say can't be done.' He then listed Australia's last 10 individual swimming gold medallists: 1968 Lyn McClements, Mike Wenden; 1972 Shane Gould, Gail Neall, Bev Whitfield, Brad Cooper; 1980 Michelle Ford; 1984 Jon Sieben; 1988 Duncan Armstrong; 1992 Kieren Perkins. Alongside 1996 was a line of question marks and the question, 'Who will be next?'

The saying is really smart because basically I went into the race with the feeling people didn't expect me to win. It was also inspirational because, again, it gave me the challenge of winning Australia's first swimming gold and joining the names of such legends. I put the paper in my tracksuit pocket, where it remained when I walked out for my moment of truth.

AN OLYMPIC GOLD MEDAL STEP BY STEP

The advantage of support

Everyone looks for an edge when facing their challenge and there's no greater bonus than having your own support crew. It's reassuring to know you're not on your own but are backed by people who've made sacrifices for you and believe in you. It gives you an extra reason for wanting to achieve, not only for yourself but also for your supporters.

It's ironic how my success has coincided with my relationship with Cliff Fairley. A lot of people have jokingly given him the credit for turning around my swimming career. I started going out with him at the end of 1994 when my times began to improve. Obviously Scott has been the one who has made the big difference with my swimming but I think Cliff has helped as well, mostly by his wonderful support. I wanted to thank him for his support and strength because I knew I wouldn't be preparing for my moment of truth, the 200m butterfly, without him. He helped me by sometimes coming to my pool and gym sessions leading to the Olympics and away from training we rarely talked about swimming. Having spent long hours qualifying to be a doctor, he showed great understanding to the commitment required to be successful at the Olympics. He helped me enjoy swimming again and no matter how stressful the situation, he could always help me relax.

Cliff arrived on the first day of the Olympic competition. From then on I either spoke to or saw him every day, and when I was lucky sometimes both. He was part of my support crew, which included my brother John and his wife Bronwyn, their friend Georgia Hume and my cousin Greg Rudolph.

I would recommend a support crew to everyone. They were so good to have around. It was difficult to make contact with them at the pool because the area was roped off and guarded by security, but we were able to say hello. It was great to see them in the stand just before I swam and I rang them a few times. Cliff and I spoke briefly about swimming but mainly it was small talk, because I needed a break away from thinking and talking about swimming.

My support crew couldn't come to my 200m butterfly heat. When I was on my way to the race I saw some phones in the walkway leading to the pool. I surprised Cliff by ringing him half-an-hour before my heat. He couldn't believe I could call him just before one of the biggest races of my life and then be so relaxed. It was unreal to feel so relaxed but I realised Cliff's support was one of the reasons for it. Again, the light conversation was a good distraction.

After my heat swim I returned to the village, had a snack, some sleep and then attended a team meeting. When I went back to the pool I caught up with my support crew again before I did my warm-up. I think Cliff felt more nervous than I did. He couldn't eat much all week and in the video of the race, he looks really pale and drawn. Mum and Dad were the same at the 1992 Olympic Games and the 1994 Commonwealth Games. It's hard when you have no control over the outcome and you want your loved one to do well.

So we met about two hours before my 200m butterfly final. There was a lot of small talk and we definitely didn't talk about the race. Cliff had earlier given me a card for the race. It was funny on the outside and inside he had written a good luck message which finished with 'PS. If your arms fly-off you've still got me, if that's any consolation'.

I have no doubt my support crew contributed to helping me

produce my best. They were a real comfort and never once put any pressure on me to win the gold medal. It was great just to know they were there and no matter how I swam they would always support me.

Preparing for your toughest rivals

Always keep the focus on your own performance but, at the same time, be ready for your main challengers. Being aware of them often gives you motivation to train and race harder. Always remember, do not fear your rivals but you need to respect them if you want to beat them.

China's form for the 1996 Atlanta Olympics was a mystery. FINA had stepped up out-of-competition testing and the Chinese had been shamed after the mass of positive tests, but this didn't guarantee the trend of the past five years would change. I had been drug tested every two to four weeks in the three months leading to Atlanta but I didn't know how strict the Chinese drug testing was. Coming into Atlanta the Chinese remained my main competition. Most of their top-named swimmers were not included in their 1995 World Short Course Championship team and many people feared this was because they were planning a big campaign for Atlanta.

It seemed the increased pressure by FINA had worked at the Atlanta Olympics, however. The Chinese under-performed there so the evidence pointed at them being on drugs when they recorded those amazing times at the 1994 World Championships. When they didn't dominate in 1996 it answered everyone's question about the drug situation.

But then came Ireland's Michelle Smith. Michelle had recorded some amazing improvements in the four years leading to Atlanta, which aroused the suspicions of the swimming world. No world class swimmer had ever been exceedingly faster at 26 years of age than at 22 until Michelle in Atlanta. Her improvement in the 400m individual medley was incredible. In

1992 she swam 4:58.94, in 1993 it was 4:57.17, in 1994 4:47.89, in 1995 4:42.81 and then she won in Atlanta with a 4:39.18 swim. A 20-second improvement in four years, including a nine-second improvement between 1993 and 1994. She hadn't competed internationally in the 400m freestyle before but in Atlanta she swam 4:07.25 – the ninth best time ever by a woman.

I hadn't noticed Michelle before, even though she finished fifth in the 200m butterfly final at the 1994 World Championships, but I know I would have remembered had she been like she was in Atlanta. She was very muscular.

I remember thinking in Atlanta, Finally the Chinese are clean and here comes another one who is suspected of being on drugs. Interestingly, I received a legal threat after saying on Brisbane radio after the Olympics that Michelle's performance suggested she was on drugs. A man with an Irish accent rang my dad's work and threatened legal action if I said publicly again she was on drugs. Obviously it's very sad and unfair how Michelle has been treated by the public and swimming world if she didn't use drugs. Everyone presumed she was on drugs and I feel sorry for her if she wasn't, but if she did cheat she deserves everything that's happened to her.

Michelle surprised everyone by winning the 400m individual medley on the first day. I found out a couple of days later her main event coming into the Olympics was the 200m butterfly. Scott started to point Michelle out to me in races. That is one of his ways of keeping me focused on the 200m butterfly, by pointing out the opposition. Constantly reminding me a win will not be easy but there will be a lot of contenders. Now I was aware of Michelle I waited to see how she went in other events. In the butterfly legs of the 200m and 400m medley events her stroke looked atrocious but she split some really, really fast time. I couldn't help but think about Michelle. Here was my first competition when the Chinese weren't swimming amazing times and I was thinking it was my best chance for a gold medal, and then all of a sudden Michelle comes out of the blue and is swimming off her tree.

Michelle Smith won the 400m freestyle after the International Olympic Committee overruled FINA, the world's swimming governing body, and allowed Michelle a late entry. Defending champion Janet Evans qualified in ninth position, so she just missed the final. Janet was involved in a controversial press conference when she was questioned about Michelle and the drug rumours. She said that naturally when people make 20-second improvements in less than four years there are going to be questions and doubts raised.

It was funny because every afternoon we would go to the pool for training and the talk around poolside was someone had been caught and there was going to be a special drug announcement. Everyone said it was Michelle Smith who had been caught. We were waiting and waiting but no announcement ever came. Then the next day the same thing would happen. There was to be a special announcement and this time it would be Michelle but, again, there was nothing. The rumour mill was churning fast about Michelle.

Then finally the day arrived for the 200m butterfly. Michelle was in the same heat as me and I was worried about her. The 200m butterfly is the only event I feel I can go easy in in the heats and still make the finals. I swam a 2:09 and secured Lane 4 as the fastest qualifier for the final and gained some confidence. For all the other races I have to do an absolute effort in the heats just to make the finals. For the 200m freestyle I had just scraped into Lane 8 and Lane 2 in the 100m butterfly.

After the 200m butterfly heat I knew I was swimming well. Michelle seemed to struggle. I felt I could pull away from her on the last lap. I felt so good I felt I could play games with the other swimmers but then I wondered if Michelle was playing a game with me. Although I won my heat fairly easily I still didn't trust the situation.

I knew Michelle could pull anything out for the final. She had looked pretty ordinary in the heat swim of the 200m individual medley but then had stormed home and won the final. In fact, she almost pulled out of the 200m individual medley, after reports of a shoulder injury, to concentrate on the 200m butterfly.

Michelle was also on a special mission. She was attempting to equal the women's record for individual swimming gold medals (four) won in an Olympics. Kristin Otto of East Germany, in 1988, was the last swimmer to accomplish the feat.

As with all my toughest rivals it was good to be aware of them and to respect them but I made sure my confidence was never rattled. I had kept tabs on Michelle's rapid rise and I knew, despite China's poor form in Atlanta, that I couldn't afford to let my guard down against longtime rival and world champion Limin Liu, who was relegated to Lane 8 in the final. She was still capable of victory so I never discounted her. At the heats in Rome she swam pretty slowly and then was able to pull out an excellent swim for the final. I had been denied so many times by the Chinese that I knew I couldn't afford to relax on this occasion. I still carried angry and painful memories about what happened at the 1994 World Championships.

But I felt this time I was ready to race and beat the drug rumours. I had worked on the last lap after the 200m butterfly final at the 1994 World Championships when I was left behind by the two Chinese. In Atlanta I knew I had done the training to make a winning challenge in the last lap. So I had strengthened my mental and physical approach which gave me the extra confidence for the Chinese swimmers and the new threat, Michelle Smith.

No way was I going to fall into the trap of paying too much attention to drug rumours at the Olympics like I did at the 1994 World Championships. I had gained such belief and focus that now I welcomed the challenge of the Chinese or anyone else on drugs because with the right preparation I was doing comparable times to their 1994 drug-assisted efforts. I was prepared for my toughest rivals.

Preparing for the final hour

There is no doubt the final hour before a major event is probably the most difficult and demanding time of the whole challenge. Make sure you surround yourself with the tools and people that will get you in the right frame of mind and focus.

I went through different stages of emotion throughout the day. I was nervous, excited or relaxed and sometimes all three rolled into one if that's possible. But in the final hour before the race I knew I needed to relax. I listened to Sting's CD 'Mercury Falling' in my room just before I left for my race. Now when I listen to the CD, it reminds me of waiting for my race.

INSPIRATIONAL NOTES

1991 Pan Pacs: Listening to AC/DC's 'Thunderstruck' fired me up to break the minute for the first time in the 100m butterfly.
1992 Olympics: By 1992 I followed a more relaxing influence to help calm my nerves. Billy Joel's 'She's Always a Woman' was a favourite.
1993 World Short Course: Mr Wakefield gave me the *Sliver* movie soundtrack for my birthday, another relaxing CD.
1994 World Championships: Counting Crows continued the mellow theme.
1995 Pan Pacs: Scott Volkers discovered Hootie and the Blowfish and whenever I think of my personal best swim in the 200m butterfly, I think of the group's first CD.
1996 Olympics: Sting's 'Mercury Falling' plus Celine Dion's 'Power of a Dream' were my Atlanta musical inspirations.

When I walked out of the room, the countdown until my race was almost complete. I couldn't help but think I could be a gold medallist the next time I walked into the room.

Once I got to the pool I met with my support crew and then I had my warm-up. After the warm-up I chatted with Scott. He told me to concentrate on the black T-bar at the end of the pool. He also reminded me to focus on my stroke. He told me to worry only about myself and my race plan and not Michelle Smith or the Chinese or anybody else. I sat with Scott while I waited for my race and I remember saying to him how really nervous I felt. With the 200m butterfly I like to be more relaxed. When I'm nervous I go out too fast because it feels easy. I just swim on adrenalin and run out in the final 50 metres and lose control on the last lap. I needed to be relaxed so I could control the race.

I started to get nervous when I thought, this is one of the biggest events of my life. I imagined myself standing behind the blocks and thinking, Oh my God, and panicking. Scott was really good and distracted me with small talk. I had never wanted to win so much in my life. That's why I'd changed coaches. That's why I'd suffered the pain of my hardest ever training program and made every sacrifice possible. Now my moment of truth had arrived and things seemed to be on track. I knew I was swimming well and I had a good chance to win gold. I knew the people around me had to swim fast to beat me.

I was heading off to the marshalling area and Scott called me back. He said, 'If you win, remember to get excited.' It was a weird thing to say but Scott was just looking after me and making sure I would show emotion for the cameras. But this was one race I didn't need a reminder for.

I usually don't feel like talking in the marshalling area but before that race was the most I've ever talked. I knew I didn't have to worry about the American swimmer, Trina Jackson, because she said to me, 'Come on, you can beat this Irish slut'.

I was really surprised but I suppose everyone was expecting Michelle to win again. So many people in the B Final said, 'Come on, you can beat her'. It was an Us versus Her feeling. It really boosted my confidence when Trina came up and supported me like that. I thought, Well I only have to beat six other finalists now.

It was bizarre. It was the most relaxed marshalling area I've been in. Everyone was relaxed and chatting about where they were going out that night. The TV screen was there and my support crew were up in the stand with their painted faces and T-shirts. I was pointing them out to the other competitors in the marshalling area. It felt more like a Brisbane Swimming Association carnival than the Olympics. Usually before an Olympic race everyone just sits there and there's no talking. In Barcelona everyone was fiddling with their goggles or peering around and seeing what each other was doing.

The marshalling was a revelation because for years I had adhered to a quiet and intense wait before my race. Never have I been so relaxed for my race and it was exactly what I needed because I didn't need to sit there and just think about my race. I already knew what I had to do. By the time you reach that final stage before a race, you already know your strategy. If you do need more preparation time then you are never going to be ready. In many ways you need to be distracted from the enormity of the situation. A calm and relaxed focus will triumph over uncontrollable nerves. The marshalling area then became even weirder.

We were about to march out when Michelle said, 'My goggles are broken. Can you hold up the race because I haven't got a spare pair of goggles.' The races are all specially timed for television. The marshal said the race had to go ahead as planned so we marched out without Michelle. I wasn't sure if she had done it on purpose, in an effort to disrupt everyone's focus on the race. When we reached the pool deck I was conscious Michelle wasn't there. I said to myself, 'She's going to turn up, so don't let it affect you.' I kept my focus and didn't worry about it and I think she ended up using borrowed goggles.

The race

The big event has arrived. You are past the preparation and training stage but you know all the hard work to reach this point will give you a headstart. The only thing you can carry with you to the starting line is the self-focus to remain firm to your assignment and the self-belief you can conquer any challenge to succeed.

We walked out and the American crowd was cheering loudly as usual but of all the nights it was probably the most like a home crowd I experienced at the Atlanta Olympics. It was great to see so many Australians in the crowd.

Scott had been working on the mindset I was getting faster as the week continued. Since changing to Scott I had done my best times on the first day of competitions and the only best time I did at the Atlanta Olympics I did on the first day as well. So the tiredness factor seems to come into competitions.

In Atlanta, however, I was glad I had a lot of swims. I felt so comfortable and relaxed in the competition environment by the time I lined up for my last race. When I watch the video I get more nervous than I did in the race. Watching the video I think, Oh my God, look at that massive crowd and the huge stands. At the time I didn't think anything of it. The crowd may as well not have even been there I was so accustomed to the setting.

I looked up to the grandstand and my support crew. They were dancing around and being idiots, which really relaxed me. Here I was about to swim probably the most important race in my life, and for them it was just entertainment.

I always have a set procedure before my races of going to the side of the pool, scooping some water in my mouth and spitting it out. But for some reason I didn't do it for the 200m butterfly final. I don't know why. Usually my mouth is dry from being so nervous it just becomes a habit. The only other superstitious thing is that I always take a couple of spare pairs of goggles and caps. But I've never needed to use them in all my years of competition.

I couldn't believe how calm I felt. I'd thought I'd be really, really nervous because this is the race I had been training for for such a long time. Instead, I felt calm and confident, as though I knew I was going to swim well. I remembered what Dawn Fraser said about attitude: 'That people have to swim pretty fast to beat me.'

Some people can smile when their names are announced before the race. There's no way I could crack a smile at that stage. Probably because I am so focused but also because it doesn't seem like the right moment: standing in front of the blocks, ready for the biggest race of my life. It seems almost fake to smile. I'm not feeling happy before a race, it's after the race I'm hoping to be happy.

People have asked me what I thought about on the blocks. All I can remember was standing on the blocks and when they blew the whistle, just thinking, Ah well, here it goes. Then I dived in and said to myself, 'Loose as a goose' to help me get into a stroke rhythm quickly.

Scott had told me to think of the race as four 50 metre races. So I swam to the end of the wall and just concentrated on the black T at the end. That's all I focused on. I never looked around. I concentrated on myself because I knew I couldn't control anyone else's movements. I knew that Michelle would swim fast but I never knew where she was for the whole race. From her previous races, the third lap has been her fast one and when you look back at the video that's when she made her move. I felt pretty fresh with one lap to go and I didn't feel like a piano had landed on top of me as in Barcelona. When I turned for the final lap and I seemed to be in front and, as it turned out, also under world record pace, I didn't get too excited. I wanted to show people I had a strong finish and this time I wouldn't shrink before my moment of truth.

I knew I was in front of the two next to me but I couldn't see Limin, so I didn't worry about positions. Once you start worrying about other swimmers passing you, that's when you start to hurt. And then they do pass you. So I kept focusing on what I had to do because I knew the race wasn't over until I touched the wall. Scott always told me I didn't have to swim faster in the last lap but just maintain what I've done.

I tried not to rush my strokes because you can get into a bad habit of tightening up when you force a sprint to the wall. I concentrated on keeping my stroke, relaxing and looking to the T-bar. It was important to focus on my double-breathing, especially in the final 25 metres. Focusing on my breathing helped me to feel strong and overcome the pain when it set in during those final strokes. It's funny how when you win, you never feel the pain.

I hit the wall and was only 70 per cent sure I was the first to touch. It was one of my favourite moments when I turned around and looked up to the scoreboard and saw I had won.

I won in 2:07.76. I was slightly disappointed it wasn't a personal best. Australian team-mate Petria Thomas was second in 2:09.82 and Michelle Smith was third, 2:09.91. Petria and I were the only people to beat Michelle in Atlanta.

And then I thought, Quick, look excited. But this time I didn't have to look excited. I was more than excited, I was ecstatic. The hard work had paid off and I had achieved my goal. At that moment, I didn't really care what other people thought. I wanted to enjoy myself. I had thought if I ever won at the Olympics I would throw my arms in the air. I couldn't practise winning in training but I had no problem throwing my arms up to celebrate in that special moment.

After the race there was a big cheer and the stadium was

buzzing. Then I looked up into the stand and all the Aussies were singing, 'One-two, one-two' for Petria and myself. Just about every Australian swimmer had finished their Olympic program so there were a lot in the stands that night. A few of the Aussies were painted in green and yellow zinc and they looked funny.

But I think my favourite moment was when I first climbed out of the pool. My support crew were standing and pumping their arms up above their heads so I stood there and pumped my arms up and down with them. You should see the video they took of the race. In the first three laps you can see me clearly and then by the last lap the video is bouncing up and down. Suddenly you see their feet and then you see the Aussie flags they are holding in the air. They were so busy cheering they forgot about filming.

The winning sensation was unbelievable, it's something now that I crave. It's like an addiction. Just to get that feeling again of winning a gold medal in front of all those people. I've watched the video a few times and I hope I get the chance to do it again. It's the biggest buzz I've ever had. And it's weird because the buzz takes you up and down. The next day, the following weeks and even months later I kept thinking, Oh my God, I've actually won. But honestly, the major feeling after winning gold was just relief.

The whole thing was better than I imagined; the whole package of the race, the presentation and having my support crew there. It superseded anything I had envisaged. It was no longer a dream which existed in my head, but it had become real that night.

Post-race

The main advice for when your event is finished is to be both gracious as a winner or loser. Always remember history is permanent but the future is not, so take motivation from your event into your future challenges. The first person I saw after my race was Elli Overton and I felt a bit bad. She had done almost exactly the same training as me the two years we were training together and she even led a lot of my sets. I think that night it really hit her the Olympics were over and she didn't fulfil her dream. She and Sam were both crying. I had mixed emotions. I was really happy I'd won but I wished Elli and Sam could have done it as well.

Then the Australian team's media manager Ian Hanson came up to me and said Channel 7 wanted me to go into the studio for an interview, which was fine. But then, when Kieren won his race, Ian came up to me and said Channel 7 didn't want me to come into the studio any more. This was also fine, because I would rather go out and celebrate.

Before our presentation we were given a mirror and comb. I parted my hair and I thought I looked a million dollars. But apparently back at home Dad wasn't too impressed because he thought my parted wet hair made me look like a boy. But who cares, I won a gold medal. From the preparation room we walked around the pool to the podium. I remember standing there hearing my name announced–'And the winner of the 200m butterfly is . . . ' and my heart started beating so fast. I stepped up and received my medal and shook hands with everybody.

I just remember standing on the dais with a feeling of disbelief. Over the years I had heard inspirational talks from Olympic gold medallists describing what it was like to win and to stand on the dais. Suddenly it was happening to me. I could hear their voices coming back to me and it was just how they described it and more.

Then the flag was raised and I couldn't believe it was happening. I didn't cry. I didn't see how anyone could cry because I was so happy. I felt on top of the world. My only grievance was that it all happened too quickly.

On the podium I remembered the card Sam's boyfriend, Johann Koss, gave me before I left for Atlanta. It was a good luck card with an Australian scene on the front. Inside the cover was the national anthem and Johann had drawn an arrow pointing to it with the words, 'Make sure you learn this because you will be singing it in Atlanta'. His thoughtful words had come true. But when it actually came to singing the national anthem I panicked because I couldn't remember all the words. I was rusty because I hadn't rehearsed it and I hadn't sung it for ages.

After the presentation we walked around the pool and stood in front of my support crew and I could only get close enough to shake everyone's hands. I wanted to give Cliff a kiss but I couldn't reach him. It was paparazzi fever. Cameras were clicking and photographers were saying stop here and stop there.

Don Talbot believes the win was my career turning point. He said he felt my Barcelona race was like a stroll in the park while the Atlanta victory was a 'show-stopping sprint'. I had overcome all the obstacles–the Chinese and Michelle Smith–but most importantly, my lack of self-belief. He said everyone in Atlanta thought Michelle would win but I showed them.

At the press conference a lot of the questions were directed at Michelle because of the drug accusations, so I mainly sat back and listened. At one stage Michelle said she would have won the race if she hadn't swum so many races during the week. She said she was tired in the race. I thought to myself, What do you think I've been doing all week? Sunbaking? I had a race on almost every day and had completed 10 races to her eight.

I was shocked when she said that because she was making excuses. I know she had some longer races than me but we both had a heavy schedule. Actually there was an article from Ireland written several months later in which the author wrote if Michelle had not broken her goggles she may have won a fourth gold medal.

The press conference was funny because I had won the gold

medal and everyone was talking to Michelle. I suppose she was the story of the week, and I didn't mind not being the centre of attention. The win was doubly satisfying because everyone had said Michelle was unbeatable. It makes it even more satisfying if she was on drugs. But a win is a win whether she was on drugs or not.

In 1997 Mum and Dad were in Ireland. When the locals heard their daughter had beaten Michelle, they said I must have been a good swimmer because Michelle was an extremely good swimmer. Mum and Dad said Michelle was very popular in Ireland and received a lot of support from the locals. Her popularity is helped because she speaks the native tongue. The locals told my parents they hated the Americans because of the drug accusations.

After the immediate presentation and celebration came the drug testing. It was such a glamorous way of spending my initial moments of joy. I go to the toilet so much while I'm waiting for my race that I find it difficult to go after my race because I'm so dehydrated. It's pretty degrading. I'd just won a gold medal and wanted to make some phone calls home and enjoy the special moment and here I was in the toilet.

It took me two hours to give a drug sample. My race was the first event on the program and Kieren's race was the last and it took me all that time. It's funny Kieren and I have our main events on the same day. Whatever I do, Kieren always seems to equal or better it. Mr Wakefield always said if I ever did well, then he knew Kieren would swim well because we always shared success on the same day.

In the 1992 Olympics and 1994 Commonwealth Games and World Championships, Kieren has won the 1500m and twice broken a world record after my 200m butterfly gold or bronze medal performances. Sometimes I get frustrated and wish I was swimming on a different day because a lot of people have said to me, 'Oh, I'll never forget Kieren's race'. I respect and admire what Kieren has done but I always think to myself, Well I swam that night as well.

Australia didn't fire in the pool until the last day. By then Australia had increased its tally to two gold, four silver and six bronze after Daniel Kowalski won the silver medal in the 1500m and then Australia won a bronze medal in the 4 x 100m men's medley relay.

I wish the Olympic program would be changed because I don't like swimming on the last day, whether Kieren is swimming or not, because most of the team are finished and are partying. It's just like if your exams are on the last day and everyone else is celebrating, which makes it harder to stay focused. But my race was over and now I could join in the celebrations.

ROLE MODELS

One of the biggest buzzes when I won an Olympic gold medal was realising the amazing history I had become part of. In the following week Australian swimming greats Michael Wenden and John Devitt welcomed me into the gold medal club and it was then I realised Australia's proud swimming history, especially for women.

I became the first Queensland woman and only the tenth Australian woman to win an individual Olympic swimming gold medal. An Australian woman had not won gold in the pool since Michelle Ford at the 1980 Olympics. It certainly is a special club to be a member of and it's so overwhelming it takes a while to sink in.

Few sports can boast such a history of female achievements, which can be tracked back to Australia's first female Olympians. Swimmers Fanny Durack and Mina Wylie fought a tough battle for women to compete at the Olympics, way back in 1912. They had a difficult time when both men and women protested about them competing at the Stockholm Olympics, the first time women's swimming events were featured. It was in an age when women were not allowed to be seen in their swimmers in front of men because it was considered morally wrong. But fortunately Fanny and Mina also had a lot of supporters, including the New South Wales Swimming Association, which set up a public fund when the Olympic fund ran out of money after paying for more than 20 men to compete for Australia.

Fanny was very independently spirited and determined. It's not surprising she went on to win the gold medal, in world record time, with Mina achieving the silver. Fanny and Mina received media attention and their brave efforts to compete at the Olympics made the road easier for other female swimmers. Australia has since produced champions such as Dawn Fraser and Shane Gould, so it has become traditional for the country's best female swimmers to receive recognition. It's not surprising that many of Australia's female role models have been swimmers like Dawn, Shane and Tracey Wickham. Australia has very few female sports role models, and it's only recently I have realised women have struggled for media space. Even in the bookshops there aren't many books written about sportswomen. I can't remember having any role models when I was growing up, but I hope I can be a role model for kids to look up to. Many people still think sport, especially swimming, may not be feminine. Some mothers fear that if their daughters compete in the 200m butterfly, they are going to turn into great hulks. But now people are realising sportswomen can be feminine, and not big and butch. Cathy Freeman, Melinda Gainsford and Sam Riley are examples of role models for girls today.

I don't swim for women's power or anything like that, but I like to see women's sport getting recognition and I will do anything to help. It's great there are now awards and groups set up to help sportswomen get recognition, and that recognition for women is increasing worldwide. There were 40 per cent more women competing in Atlanta than Barcelona because of the introduction of sports such as softball and women's soccer. The 200m butterfly wasn't added to the women's program until 1968, 12 years after the men first swam the event. In fact, my winning time in 1996 would have won the men's final at the 1968 Olympics.

In Fanny Durack's day being a female swimmer was a burden and now, more than 80 years later, I haven't encountered a problem with media and public recognition. The support after my Olympic win has been incredible and I'm still coming to terms with being grouped with such golden legends as part of Australia's Olympic swimming tradition.

Celebrating

Celebration is an important and natural part of any big event or challenge, whether you have been successful or not. It's healthy to unwind and relax after all the work you've put into the challenge. You need to have a mental and physical break so you will be recharged and ready for the next challenge.

Everything happened so fast the night I won and I remember waking up the next day and being suddenly hit with the realisation I had won. There was another press conference and it was pouring on our return to our rooms. So we thought because we were already soaked we would jump into the fountains in our tracksuits. So Sam, Nicole and myself were among those who decided to have fun in the fountains and swim around in our tracksuits. It was great to behave like idiots after all the tension and stress of the past week.

In the second week of the Olympics I checked out of the team and stayed with Cliff. I slept heaps, went shopping and then partied at night. I also saw a lot of Sam and Elli. I was enjoying the feeling I had done everything I had aimed to do. I don't think what I had achieved really sank in until the second week when I had time to think about it.

One day before the competition started the Australian team had gone out shopping. Channel 7 were there and were asking questions. Somebody asked me what I would do if I won a gold medal. I told them I would buy the whole shopping centre. And I pretty much did that.

A couple of days after the race my support crew and I went shopping. It was excellent. I would stand in the change room and they'd throw over clothes and I'd put them on and they would say yes or no, to whether they suited me or not. We all walked out of the shops with armfuls of bags full of newly bought goodies for me. No one could believe the bags were all mine because I've never been known as a big shopper.

A week after the swimming finished, actually my twenty-third birthday, somebody had heard about a special day for medallists at Centennial Park. It was unbelievable to walk out in front of a huge crowd, about 100,000 people. All the American medallists were saying 'Yeah!' and really going off. And then Sam and I walked up and we did this small 'Hi'. Thankfully the crowd cheered just as loud for us as they did for the Americans, which was really nice.

The closing ceremony was great. We got there a couple of hours beforehand and we all sat together as a team. Everyone got into a big paper fight. Everyone was ripping up the program we had been given. While we were waiting for the ceremony to start we had a massive paper fight with the Netherlands team. It was so much fun.

Closing ceremonies are always memorable. All the competition and the accompanying tension are over and everyone is relaxed and can be as silly as they like. During the closing ceremony one of the athletes down the front suddenly realised the security guards were doing a conga line instead of holding their usual position around the oval. Then some of the athletes down the front got up and raced to the stadium oval and then a whole heap of athletes streamed down onto the oval, including myself.

The performers, like Little Richard and Gloria Estefan, were still out there. We saw Little Richard close up and he had all this make-up on and it was dripping off his face. Everyone was dancing around and I did some cartwheels. All the athletes were friends that night. We were all on the biggest high.

I remembered the Barcelona closing ceremony when the big scoreboard came up with 'See you in Atlanta'. Well, now Atlanta was over and I'd won a gold medal. This time the scoreboard said 'See you in Sydney'. I wonder what Sydney holds?

Now, whenever I feel depressed with swimming or with life or I'm generally feeling down, I think about Atlanta and winning the gold medal and it really lifts me. The closing ceremony was also one of the highlights.

When we had to leave the village it was a really empty feeling. It was absolutely pouring down rain and the atmosphere became eerie, with the once vibrant village now empty and in the path of lightning and a storm. We ran out to the buses. At the back of the bus I turned around to look at the village one more time. After four weeks of buzzing activity, it was empty, like a ghost town.

CHAPTER
FOCUS

- Everyone looks for an edge when facing their challenge and there is no greater bonus than having the support of people who have made sacrifices for you.

- Always keep the focus on your own performance. Respect, but don't fear your main challengers.

- Whether you win or lose, you should always be gracious.

- After every hard-earned, tiring and long-fought campaign, whether it is only partly or fully successful, it is important to have a mental and physical break before beginning the next challenge.

PART FOUR

Reaching the dais

My success in Atlanta created a whole lot of new and interesting scenarios. I was at the start of a new chapter and learning to handle this sudden world of praise and expectations. By the end of 1996 I was diving into a new pool, with a new set of self-doubt and challenges to overcome.

Being an Olympic champion did not mean I stopped making mistakes. I had to learn about many things including performing with the expectation which accompanies an Olympic title, before finding a new set of goals. 1998 proved one of my most challenging years starting with the world championships in January in Perth where I won my first ever world title, followed by the public frenzy of the Commonwealth Games where there was heavy expectation I would win a record ten gold medals. The Games was the breakthrough competition where I entered the 'zone' for the first time, a skill which helped me break a world record as I continue to learn how to reach the top of the medal dais again and again.

4

CHAPTER TEN

REWARD

'Success is never final; failure is never fatal.'
JOE PATERNO

'To win takes a complete commitment of
mind and body. When you can't make that
commitment, they don't call you a champion
any more.' **ROCKY MARCIANO**

We had just boarded the plane in Atlanta for home when Australian Olympic Committee president John Coates came up to me and asked if I would like to sit in first class. I didn't know what to do because I wanted to sit with my team-mates but it was also good to have more leg room and I didn't want to say no to Mr Coates. So I went up to first class, which ended up being pretty good and I was able to get some sleep for the journey home.

But moving to first class came at a price. Just before we landed in Sydney Mr Coates said he wanted me to give a short speech to our expected big welcome. He wanted me to thank everybody for sending faxes and messages. I became nervous.

In the past I could simply hop off the plane and slip into the crowd. But I realised I was no longer seen as the same person as I was when I had left for Atlanta two months before. I had travelled to Atlanta with the self-belief and self-focus that I could achieve my goal of an Olympic gold, but it is an entirely different proposition when you have achieved that. You don't receive a gold medal alone but all the attention and accolades that come with it. On my way home I realised I had become an Olympic champion on a very public stage, so a large part of my win would become public property.

The two chartered planes full of Olympic athletes and officials were steered into a special hangar at Sydney airport and parked next to each other. Many of the athletes' families were there and when we disembarked there was a singer belting out the chorus of 'Advance Australia Fair'. It was an unbelievable welcome home. Myself and Mike McKay, from the Oarsome Foursome, then had to give a speech, which was quite nerve-racking knowing there were people like Prime Minister John Howard in the audience. Welcome to my new life as an Olympic gold medallist.

1988 Olympic gold medallist Debbie Flintoff-King had warned me in Atlanta my life would change. She was right. But

I have treated it as a positive because I have learnt so much since I won an Olympic gold medal, such as developing the skill of speaking in public. Don Talbot told me I had changed since becoming an Olympic champion, but for the better. He said I wasn't as simple as I used to be, which he meant in the nicest possible way. Don believes 1996 was a turning point for me. He thinks I have become more extroverted, more self-confident and more conscious of my ability now I have an Olympic title to my name.

Since I've won the gold medal my life has certainly become a lot busier, which is great. I've had a lot more opportunities. People have wanted to talk to me at functions. When you are an up-and-coming swimmer no one really knows you and while it's good to have that anonymity, it's also been good to get recognition. Success is a double-edged sword. You like and want recognition but at the same time it can be hard to deal with sometimes.

I've never felt like I've lived in a goldfish bowl or a protected cage. I'm occasionally recognised or stopped in shopping centres. Sometimes it's hard when you don't feel like talking but generally people have been very supportive. It's something which takes getting used to but I'm sure leading to the Sydney Olympics it is something I'll become more familiar with. Most people are good and are rarely intrusive. I've never had a problem relaxing in public forums such as at the beach or at the movies.

Ninety-nine per cent of fan mail has been fantastic. I received several thousand letters after Atlanta and signed every return letter, which took me well into 1997. I feel it's important to take the time out to send the letters myself, because I know everyone would want a reply after spending the time to send me a letter. I think if I ever got heaps and heaps of letters I would just take out a newspaper advertisement to thank everybody because it would be impossible to answer them all.

Unfortunately success sometimes has its intrusive price, such as when I've received the occasional negative letter. There are lots of stories about athletes and celebrities who've received unwanted attention. I wouldn't receive such attention if I wasn't in the public eye. But it's disappointing because all I do is swim. I'm not a terrorist or an assassin. I haven't done anything to hurt anybody. Just because I am in the public eye doesn't mean I deserve to be harassed. I'm just trying to swim my best for Australia.

Truthfully, there have been a couple of times I've wished I hadn't won the gold medal. That thought has lasted for only a millisecond. I'm naturally a pretty private person, so enjoying the spotlight doesn't come naturally. I occasionally thought about giving my medal back when I was really tired after an overload of functions. There was an exhausting amount of event and media demands after the Olympics, especially in December 1996, around the time of many award dinners. At some functions I felt pressure that people expected me to be perfect in all aspects of my life, now I was an Olympic gold medallist.

Sometimes I feel I'm still coming to terms with the thought I am an Olympic champion. Some days I wake up and think, Wow I've won a gold medal! I strove for years to win a gold medal and it seems it will take a similar timeframe for the achievement to sink in. Other days I wonder what all the fuss is about. I think, All I did was swim four laps faster than anyone else, with my arms turning over in unison.

On days when things get too much I have a safeguard. I return to my comfort zone–the pool. Training is a great way to switch off from any outside pressures and do what I love to do best, swim.

Although the spotlight has sometimes been uncomfortable and demanding, winning the gold medal has improved my life. The day I won the gold medal was the best day of my life and 1996 has been the best year of my life. I didn't want 1996 to end but I realised I couldn't live on my past success. My life didn't stop when I won an Olympic gold medal. Now I have the determination and confidence to strive and work hard for more success. Again I choose to win.

HOW TO RIDE THE ROLLER-COASTER OF SUCCESS

It's not surprising when people who have successfully completed a challenge that has taken several months, or even years to achieve, may initially experience a high followed by a low. It's hard to resume life after you have devoted several years to completing a special project, such as a degree or a big business deal, and then suddenly the focus of all your attention is over. It's important to ride out the letdown until you find excitement in your next goal or challenge.

You always hear of athletes talking about Olympic hangovers. I got one after Atlanta. I suppose it's only natural. I'd just experienced the biggest high of my life and I had to come down sometime. But it was like a roller-coaster ride I had no control over. Sometimes I would think, Wow my life's excellent. Then the next day I would plummet down when I had no answers for what I was going to do with the rest of my life. I felt the lows when I was trying to sort out my future.

For four months there were many functions, lunches and dinners, especially in the first weeks after arriving home. I was caught up in an uncontrollable whirlwind and my lifestyle was really bizarre. I went to ticker-tape parades in Brisbane, Sydney and Melbourne.

In Atlanta I knew I had achieved something special but it wasn't until I took part in the Sydney ticker-tape parade that I realised what I'd actually achieved, when I saw the amount of people who came out for the parade. It seemed so many people had watched the Olympics and we could feel their interest and support.

The ticker-tape parade dinner in Brisbane was unreal. It was held at the City Hall and it had a relaxed and fun feeling.

Everyone had helium balloons on their tables, and suddenly a balloon with a bread roll floated past. Then there was one with a bread roll and a fork sticking out. Then someone put three balloons together and tied their medals to it and it floated across the room.

The Australian women's hockey team got up and played a song. They had a guitar and they sang. Everyone started to dance. Then someone asked me to sing so I went up on stage with a tambourine and sang into the microphone. I can't remember what I sang but unfortunately a lot of people can. I'm still being reminded about it. It was good to let my hair down.

In the four months I only had time for a two-week holiday. There were 16 of us, including myself and Cliff, and we hired two yachts in the Whitsundays. It was awesome fun. Sam Riley and Johann Koss also came and we sailed around and relaxed. Sam didn't hold me to the Olympic pact of bungy jumping after I won the gold medal. I was able to chicken out once again.

I was still on a high in December when I had to start making decisions about my future, especially whether I would return to swimming. It was after the whirlwind stopped and I found myself in the lowest valley of the roller-coaster that I had a chance to think clearly about my future. I realised a decision was required soon. It was great to relax for those few months after the Olympics, but after all those functions I wanted to fit into my clothes again. I struggled with a lack of motivation and thoughts of retiring from October 1996 to January 1997. I had to sort out what I wanted to do and I knew it was something that couldn't be resolved overnight.

I'm glad I gave myself time to make my decision and didn't push myself into anything too soon after such a dramatic high. I think if I'd returned to swimming too early it may have permanently spoilt any enjoyment I had for the sport. I had learnt the only way to persevere with an activity was to enjoy it and be hungry to complete new goals. After the highs and lows of those months I no longer wanted to ride the roller-coaster. I needed stability. The key to stability was to find another challenge. I had to find new goals to spark my competitive fire. I had to decide on a career, whether it would remain swimming or another challenge.

HANDLING MONEY MATTERS

Unfortunately so much of today's focus revolves around money, but don't use money as your prime motivation because it can often sidetrack you from your goal. To find enjoyment in your challenge you should be driven by the love of it and not by money. You also need to be able to trust your money manager that he or she is doing the best for you. Sport is so hung up about money these days. But in my humble opinion sport shouldn't be like that.

One of the reasons that helped me win the gold medal was the fact I didn't get into the money side of things until after Atlanta. Money was neither an incentive nor a distraction and I was able to focus solely on my swimming. On the other hand, I believe if you achieve something special it should be rewarded. Some of my motivational problems after Atlanta came from the lack of recognition and financial support immediately after my gold medal win.

It was a hard time for me because I'd won the ultimate in sport – a gold medal – and yet I'd attracted no major sponsors. I've never worried about swimming for money but when I was deciding whether to return to the pool I suddenly realised, What was the point of going through all that pain in training when I'd achieved no financial security despite winning gold? Financially and competitively my future was uncertain.

I was very naive about money and sports management when I first signed with IMG (International Management Group) in late 1992. It was just after my bronze medal win in Barcelona and I'd recently left school. I remember at the time thinking, 'Wow, imagine, I will be with IMG'. I was excited but not streetwise. Looking back it was ridiculous to be so excited about the name of IMG, which is one of the biggest in world sport. I didn't look past the name to make sure they would do the right thing by me.

The financial rewards didn't interest me too much. I thought I might get some minor sponsorships but it was never a motivating factor. I was swimming because I loved it and winning medals was my motivation. I never pushed the issue with IMG. I should have cared a lot more about what they were doing for me, but I floated along and trusted IMG. Frustratingly, in four years IMG got me only two sponsors, and I know that one of the companies actually approached IMG about sponsoring me.

After Atlanta the lack of recognition and sponsorship didn't worry me at first. It wasn't until a couple of months had passed, when I was deciding what to do with my life and whether I was going to keep swimming, that it suddenly hit me. I didn't have any sponsors. What was I going to live off? I had been waiting at home for something to happen and nothing did.

I contacted IMG and they told me how hard it was to get sponsors and I said, fair enough. But then I became concerned and I asked them which companies they had sent my profiles to. They hadn't sent anything out until October and I'd won my Olympic gold, silver and bronze medals in July. I realised I had to make an immediate drastic change with my financial management before it became too late to take advantage of my Olympic success.

At the same time Rob Woodhouse, a former Australian teammate and 1984 400m medley bronze medallist, happened to ring me. He first rang me before the Olympic trials to tell me he was now a sports manager. I'd told him thanks, but no thanks, I'm really happy where I am. People had warned me about IMG but I hadn't wanted to think about that sort of stuff before the Olympics when I was focusing on my gold medal goal.

Rob happened to ring me at a time when I was confused and upset about my future. I said to him, 'Thank goodness you rang. I don't know what to do with my life.' When I went to Rob it wasn't panic stations but almost, because it was five months since I had won Olympic gold, which made his job more difficult.

Rob flew to Brisbane the following day after we had talked. I thought he sounded good and he would give 100 per cent to helping me. I decided I would like to work with him and I split with IMG in December. After the split IMG's Graeme Hannan was quoted as saying I wasn't as personable or promotable as Sam Riley, which didn't hurt me but made me realise I probably should have left IMG earlier. If they thought that why did they bother to manage me? I was angry because they had been wasting my time and could have damaged my future.

Obviously I was too small for IMG. The company makes millions out of events, so why would they want to spend time on me? I just wished they'd told me the truth instead of going, 'Oh, we're trying' when they weren't doing anything. Rob has been a wonderful manager and has secured three principal sponsors with Telstra, Westpac and Westfield. I have associate sponsorships with Qantas, Speedo and Capilano Honey. Torque Ford has been a valuable sponsor by providing me with a car.

Rob took over my management at the end of the year when many awards were being announced. I was surprised to win Australian Swimmer of the Year, Female Olympian of 1996, Australian Sportswoman of the Year, Queensland Sportsperson of the Year and Queensland Young Achiever of the Year. The awards helped to generate interest from sponsors.

The money and management side of sport came as a big shock to me. I was surprised to find that often it didn't come down to your athletic ability. A lot of it had to do with having the right manager and how well he or she could project your image to sponsors. Of course, you have to have a marketable product, but at the same time it's how well you are able to sell it.

But an athlete's first concern is their sport and they should worry about the money side of things only when they have to. If you get a manager you can trust, you leave all the money worry to them. If you are looking for a manager, it's better to go with somebody smaller than a big company. It's also good to have someone who specialises with athletes, not with events. Find somebody understanding and maybe who has been an elite sportsperson themselves and knows how important the right amount of training is.

It's important to have a manager looking after you since you can't expect companies to come to you. The managers have to go to the companies and convince them why their clients would be good for their company. That's why I could never be my own manager. I could never go out and say how good I am or how much money I'm worth.

Most importantly, I'm still swimming because I love it. The difference is now I'm more realistic about the financial side of things. I have to make a living out of swimming if I want to stay in the sport, especially if I'm going to aim for the Sydney Olympics.

In the past it was impossible for somebody to make a career out of swimming, but with increased sponsorship and government support swimming could become a career. Most people my age have a job or a university degree. I have to treat swimming like a profession, but I'm fortunate I can still have fun with swimming.

If I ever stopped enjoying swimming I would retire. It was really interesting reading about Debbie Flintoff-King and how she started to run for her family and sponsors after becoming the 1988 Olympic 400m hurdles champion. When that happened her heart was no longer in her sport and consequently she didn't perform at her best. She now wishes she had retired directly after the Olympics. I never want to swim for money or for the financial benefits I can get out of the sport. I'm driven by the love of my sport.

SETTING NEW GOALS

Anyone who has ever achieved success has had a goal. You cannot move forward until you have a goal to strive for, even if it's a small goal. Doubt, depression or uncertainty can strike when you have no goal or your goal seems unrealistic. Keep your goals in portions you can manage and then enjoy the satisfaction of achieving them and moving ahead.

From October 1996 to January 1997 I couldn't help but think about retiring. One week I wanted to retire and the next I wanted to keep swimming again. The thoughts about retiring were the strongest when I started training again in December 1996. I thought, Do I want to go through all this again?

I could vividly remember the final weeks leading to Atlanta and all the pain from the hardest training I'd ever done. I remembered that I couldn't wait until it was all over and I could stop swimming. I'd gone to Atlanta with the thought that it could be my last competition, especially if I won, because I'd achieved what I'd set out to do. When I returned to training I found it such a hassle and it seemed so boring swimming lap after lap. To make things even harder I was so unfit after the longest break of my career, which meant I regularly struggled in training. But my biggest problem was I had no goal to aim for.

The retirement thoughts were particularly strong after the Queensland Titles in January. I didn't want to swim any more. I found it difficult to get back into a routine after several months of the good life and especially tough to relate to my goal of winning a gold medal at the 2000 Olympics. The Sydney Olympics seemed too far away and I didn't know how I could cope with another four years of training.

After every Olympics a lot of people who have done well never come back. They forget about the hard training that led to their success. I suppose you could be lulled into thinking you don't have to train that hard again once you've won a gold medal. You also hear of many older swimmers who lose their hunger and excitement. I understood that mentality because after Atlanta I lost my hunger and I needed the break to find it again.

Scott Volkers left it up to me to make the decision. He didn't push me but let me work through the issues myself. It was important I regained the hunger through my own efforts. If I'd come back too hard, too early, I could have lost my motivation altogether.

It wasn't until April 1997 that I felt hungry again and wanted to train full-time. I finally realised there was nothing more I enjoyed than swimming. I also knew I would have regretted it if I had retired when I felt I still hadn't reached my potential. Suddenly I found myself setting and striving for goals again.

Anyone who has ever achieved success has had a goal. I needed a goal after the Olympics and I found several goals to re-motivate myself.

THE SIX GOALS THAT KEPT ME SWIMMING

Setting a series of small goals

Obviously every Australian athlete who is currently competing would be aiming for the 2000 Olympics but after eight years in the Australian team, another four years seemed such a long way. By 1997 I had been swimming competitively for 16 years, so I needed more specific goals to help me maintain my excitement with the sport.

Instead of looking at the 2000 Olympics, I found realistic goals to keep me hungry in the years leading to Sydney. Suddenly the road to the 2000 Olympics seemed more easily digestible. My initial targets included the 1998 World Championships in Perth and the 1998 Commonwealth Games in Kuala Lumpur. After them I was so close to the Sydney Games that I could not resist the challenge, especially when I was still in good form.

Surrounding myself with hard workers

I've always been motivated by competition, whether it was in training or racing. I am fortunate that in Scott Volkers' squad there's a lot of hard workers in training, which only helps to motivate me. Kristy Ellem, a young breaststroker, is highly motivated and has a strong work ethic. Sam Riley is another hard worker who does some amazing times in training, and we motivate each other by swimming well.

Furthermore Sam, Elli Overton and I carry this dream to retire at the same time. I'm a bit worried about Elli. She's such a good swimmer but she was uncertain what to do after Atlanta so she went to study and train at a college in the United States, which worked because she made the 1998 world championship team. So for us all it's a strong motivation to keep working hard in training and to continue making teams together.

Finding motivation in keeping ahead of the upcoming competition

There are a few upcoming swimmers who are hot on my heels. I learnt from the 1993 Pan Pac Championships not to be complacent after missing the 200m butterfly final. Now teenagers such as Julia Ham and Kate Godfrey have already recorded very competitive times, while Angie Kennedy and Petria Thomas remain strong forces in butterfly.

These swimmers are particularly targeting the 100m butterfly, my second event. By 1999 I'd won ten successive 100m butterfly national titles, achieving my aim to equal Nicole Stevenson's record of ten. This was one of my short-term goals which kept me going until the 2000 Olympics, knowing it would not be easy with the increasing depth of butterfly swimming in Australia.

The 1997 World Short Course Championships in Sweden was the first Australian team I had missed since 1989. I knew the championships in April would be an ideal test to see how much I missed swimming and competing. I realised after the championships I was not ready to retire because I missed competing too much. Competitions give me an adrenalin rush and I know how hard it is to find something you can be passionate about. I found it difficult to watch the championships on television and seeing the results of other competitors motivated me to train harder. I realised there was nothing else I wanted to do as much as swim again. I must be addicted to competing. I craved to be back competing in the next Australian team. And to add to the motivation there is now a fresh bunch of hopefuls to challenge me.

Exploring a change

Often a change is a good way to renew motivation and hunger, whether it is a change of environment, coaches or events. In the past a change of event or coach has helped me overcome some career lows. After the Atlanta Olympics I was definitely happy with coach Scott Volkers but there was talk about me changing events.

The most-asked question in interviews has always been whether I am considering adding to or reducing my heavy schedule of events. Already I have three individual events (200m freestyle, 200m butterfly and 100m butterfly) and three relay events (4 x 200m, medley and 4 x 100m).

I've looked at a change of events and I think there's an international opening in the 400m freestyle. There's definitely a better chance internationally to win gold in the 400m freestyle than the 100m freestyle. But it would be difficult for me to drop the 100m butterfly and 200m freestyle because I've had considerable success with them in the past.

In the past a change of events has helped me regain my enjoyment and determination, but this time I didn't need a change to help with motivation. I realised adding the 400m freestyle wasn't possible. I swam the 400m freestyle at the 1998 Commonwealth Games but for the 2000 Olympics I realised I should be cutting down rather than adding another race.

I've always done my best 200m butterfly on the first day when I'm the freshest. Swimming in a 400m freestyle race wouldn't make me fresh. Instead, I've restricted swimming 400m freestyles to my training as part of my program to increase my stamina. But certainly, thinking about a change and setting new goals can get you excited about your work.

Finding your toughest challenge

To further regain my hunger, I needed a goal strong enough to drive me for four years. And I found this with the world's longest records in women's swimming. In August 1981, 16-year-old Mary T. Meahger of Kentucky, United States, produced such astonishing 100m and 200m butterfly swims that neither herself nor anyone else has come close to them since. She recorded 57.93 in the 100m butterfly and 2:05.96 in the 200m butterfly. They were two of the most breathtaking swims in history and, amazingly, were completed in pouring rain in the outdoor pool of Brown Deer in the United States.

At the time of writing, I was the second fastest 200m butterfly swimmer in history behind Mary. I would hate to retire without giving the long-course world record a good crack, otherwise I would always wonder if maybe I could have reached it. It was certainly a carrot to dangle in front of me to get me excited about swimming again. A long course world record is something I've never owned.

Amazingly, I've been under world record pace in several 200m butterfly races: in the 1992 Barcelona Olympics, at the 1995 Pan Pacs in Atlanta and then at the 1996 Atlanta Olympics. In the first nine months under Scott I slashed my previous personal best set in Barcelona, 2:09.03, by almost two seconds by the 1995 Pan Pacs, 2:07.29. Sometimes another 1.6 seconds seems a long way away and other times I feel close to the world record, especially after improving by almost two seconds in one swim.

I'm careful never to think about the record when I swim. You have to concentrate on your race and not on records, or otherwise you'll make mistakes. But you also have to carry the belief you can swim faster. I've only held that belief since 1995. The new belief coincided with Scott telling me I hadn't reached my potential and there was room for improvement, especially in the final 50 metres. That is such a different attitude from 1993 when I thought there was no way I could break the record. Then it had seemed unreachable and I had no chance of achieving it.

I had an interesting talk after Atlanta with Sam's boyfriend, Olympic gold medallist Johann Koss, which really had an effect on me. Johann won Olympic gold for speed skating in 1992 and then trained intensely in 1993 while he privately nursed the belief he couldn't go faster. Sure enough, he didn't go faster. Then, in 1994, he reduced his training to lead a more balanced and relaxed life and he regained the enjoyment for skating and the belief he could improve. In his hometown Winter Olympics at Lillehammer, Norway, in 1994, he set world records in winning three individual titles–the 1500m, 5000m and 10,000m speed skating events.

So much is to do with your mental attitude, and now I feel ready for my toughest challenge. You will only go faster if you believe you can. I believe I can go faster and now breaking the world record has become a realistic goal.

The lure of a special event

No event could be more special than a hometown Olympics. In 1993 Sydney was announced as the 2000 Olympic city and, at that stage, no way did I think I would still be swimming. I would be a 27-year-old swimming grandma. Everyone was screaming and celebrating the decision and I looked around and wondered who would still be around. Sam, Elli and I continue to compete, as well as Daniel Kowalski, but many of the people who celebrated that day are no longer swimming.

The next day I read in the newspaper about an unknown swimmer called Emma Johnson who listed all my events as the ones she would be swimming at the 2000 Olympics. I thought, It doesn't matter because I won't be around by then anyway. It was weird to think someone would be swimming my events. Since then everything has turned around: I'm still swimming, Emma has changed events and, of course, Emma was one of my team-mates in the 4 x 200m relay in Atlanta which won a bronze medal.

Winning a gold medal in Sydney in front of my family and an Australian crowd would surely be the ultimate, and it's become a big incentive. I've now twice swum in front of Australian crowds: at the 1991 and 1998 world swimming championships in Perth. I remember at the Commonwealth Games in Victoria that the Canadians were so scared of failure and letting down their home crowd before all their events. I'm determined not to be like that for Sydney. I won't slit my wrists if I don't do well in Sydney, but the 2000 Olympics is a driving goal at the moment.

Thinking about the gold medal swim in Atlanta lifts me and I find it helpful to draw on that. I crave another Olympic gold medal. If I have a bad session or I'm feeling low in training, Scott tells me to think about the day I won the Olympic gold medal. Now I have the goal to repeat my 1996 Olympic gold medal success in the 2000 Olympics.

LEARNING SUCCESS IS NEVER FINAL AND FAILURE IS NEVER FATAL

Once you have achieved your goal and experienced success, you can't relax. Success is never final and there are new troughs to hurdle and new peaks to climb. You have to use the skills you learnt on your original road to success as the foundations for more success. But it is impossible to always be successful. The real moment of truth comes with those who best recover from failure and disappointment. Failure is never fatal because there's always the hope of another success and goal to strive for and achieve.

After I won the gold medal at Atlanta I felt I had entered a whole new world. I found myself in a strange and sometimes uncomfortable environment. A gold medal brought new demands, new opportunities and new pressures. But instead of feeling my life had stopped after my Olympic gold medal swim, I realised I had a whole new set of challenges to conquer. While the challenges may have been different, the skills remained the same.

If I had to sum up my success in the pool I would list five keys: balance, hard work and perseverance, learn and improve, self-focus, and finally, self-belief. After I came back from Atlanta it hit me that these were the same qualities I used for the diverse challenges I faced in my new, post-Atlanta, life to achieve things I never thought would be possible. I realised it was a simple formula to help with any challenge, because everyone can choose to win.

OVERCOMING EVERYDAY CHALLENGES

Confidence in public

I've always been confident in the pool and shy out of it. For years I've simply swum and tried to avoid the external trappings of a public profile. I couldn't imagine anything worse than standing up in front of a heap of people and delivering a speech. But since I've won the gold medal I've had to do the things I once avoided, such as public speaking.

I've adapted surprisingly well to this new aspect of my life with the help of my new-found *self-belief*. But, most importantly, I now have the confidence and focus outside the pool that once was reserved only for my swimming. I've grown up since winning the gold medal and I think becoming an Olympic champion as a 23-year-old has had many advantages over winning it as a teenager. I know I am more mature and I have a better grip on handling the changes to my life.

The more public speaking I've done the more normal it has become, though I don't know if I can ever feel natural about it. It's one more facet of my life that I'm working on and trying to improve. I have vivid memories of my first television interview as a shy 14-year-old dazzled by the bright lights when I could manage only three one-word answers. After that tentative start I'm sure people would be surprised to know I am now doing quite a bit of public speaking.

Public speaking is the closest thing I've experienced to the adrenalin rush I get from swimming and competing. The best feeling is when people come up to you and want to write down one of your quotes. Then you really feel like you have helped somebody.

I'd rather speak to hundreds and hundreds of people in a company function than to a small group. I hate speaking to small groups, especially when I know most of the people in the room and many of them are my peers. I feel less pressure talking in front of people I don't know.

Some of the talks can be fun. The funniest question has been at a rugby lunch when one of the players asked me something like if it helped to have sex before sport. But probably my favourite talks are those I give at schools when I talk to kids, because kids are so honest and fun.

I've always been a shorts and T-shirt type person as my whole life revolved around swimming. Now I'm a gold medallist I have to look professional when I'm at functions, especially if I'm speaking at them, because no one would listen to somebody in their jeans.

I feel more poised and confident in the spotlight since I've won an Olympic gold medal. It's great to finally find enjoyment and success in other aspects of my life besides swimming, which has helped me to achieve a confident, happy and balanced focus.

Handling praise

When you win an Olympic gold medal suddenly you have to deal with all these accolades. I found when I attended functions people didn't stop praising me. I was conscious not to let the praise go to my head. You could easily fall into the trap of believing what everybody says and then thinking you don't have to train hard again. I realised the public response wouldn't last forever and to continue to achieve I needed to continue to work hard.

I can understand how easily success can go to someone's head, but, remember, whatever anyone has achieved, it doesn't make them a better person. I hate it when somebody is arrogant and people make excuses for them like 'Oh, they can afford to be like that because they've done this'. That's a pretty poor excuse. My parents keep me down to earth and if I say anything that sounds a bit uppity, they get stuck into me. They taught me you have to be a nice person and to be nice to others no matter what you achieve with your life.

In the past, a couple of gold medallists have suddenly become experts on everything, even if swimming was not their main sport. I was determined not to be like that. I succeeded in a swimming race but despite the victory, I didn't know everything. Even though I've won a gold medal I still had a lot to learn and there are many areas I need to improve.

I didn't suddenly hold the key to all knowledge after winning an Olympic gold medal. I learnt that to continue to be successful required the same formula as every success—*hard work* and *perseverance*. Although I have achieved the ultimate in sport, I cannot afford to be complacent and fall back on my success. To continue to succeed in swimming I have to keep up the training sessions and to apply the perseverance that took me to an Olympic gold medal after eight years in the Australian swimming team.

Balancing commitments

When you experience success, suddenly you find yourself in demand. People want to hear you speak or to advertise their products. I've learnt I can't please everybody. I've had to say no to some commitments because training comes first. It would be nice to say yes to every charity and organisation that asked for your help, but you can't. To do so there would be a danger of losing control of your focus.

Early in 1997 my training was suffering because of hectic scheduling and on some days I wasn't having my required rest. It's something I've worked on because you can't feel tired and do your best in training. Training has to come first. My sponsors are understanding about training. They realise I only became a good swimmer from disciplined training.

Once the 200m butterfly race controlled me, until I gained confidence and through hard work learnt to be in control of my favourite race. By the Atlanta Olympics I had a relaxed control before and during my race, which helped me to succeed. I applied the same formula to my scheduling. Out-of-pool commitments were important but I couldn't let them control my life. I needed to have a balance.

Handling pressure

There is an old saying that the higher you rise, the further you can fall. If you continue on this line then the more successful you become, the more pressure there will be to maintain the high standard. Success and pressure are not bogy words but should be treated as friends. Whatever success and pressure you have had in the past, you can draw and *learn* from that experience to help with your next challenge.

But there is no escaping from the fact that the spotlight and accompanying pressure are going to become more intense on Australia's best medal chances as we move towards the 2000 Olympics. In Atlanta I used two methods in handling the

Olympic-size pressure. Firstly, it came back to my *self-belief*. I was quietly confident but I never saw myself as the favourite, so I never let myself carry the pressure of being the frontrunner. It comes down to you and your expectations and no one else's. You don't have to answer to anyone but yourself. Always make sure it's everyone else's hype and expectation and not yours. I found it reassuring when Scott said, 'All I can ask is your best'. Nobody is perfect and if you can give your heart, your determination and your focus, drawing on all your potential, then nobody can ask more from you.

Secondly, *self-focus* helped me to overcome the different pressures in Atlanta. There were a lot of distractions, including medal hype, public criticism after the disappointment with Australia's swimming performances and unsettling talk about Michelle Smith and the drug suspicions. But I didn't let any of these factors affect my performance because of my self-focus. There was nothing I could do about the distractions except ignore them, so I focused on my swimming and doing what I needed to do to win.

Now, whenever I feel media hype, pressure or any other distraction getting out of control, I know I can go back to the mantra that helped me at the Atlanta Olympics. I stayed focused, believed and won.

Learning to be myself

Instead of the Olympic success going to my head it had the opposite effect. Initially, the extra attention made me feel insecure. I thought everyone expected me to be perfect in all aspects of my life and I felt pressure to succeed out of the pool. I felt being an Olympic champion, people would expect me to be a super-duper smooth-talking, super-confident person who knew everything out of the pool. I was out of my league and felt very self-conscious. This fear made it much worse when I tried to deal with the public attention. I wasn't comfortable in the spotlight. I was scared people might think I was dull and boring and not as good as what they expected. I didn't like to think I was disappointing people.

Thankfully I got over that. I may have won an Olympic gold medal but I had to learn it shouldn't change how I conducted myself out of the pool. In the pool I had gained self-belief, which took me to an Olympic gold medal. In the last 50 metres of my race, in my moment of truth, I had to focus on doing my best and believing I could win. Now I had to learn to develop that same self-belief away from the pool. I realised the secret was to just be myself and not try to be someone I wasn't.

CHAPTER
FOCUS

- There is often an initial high after achieving a long-term challenge, followed by a letdown when the focus of all your attention is over. Ride out the letdown until you find excitement in your next goal or challenge.

- To find enjoyment in your challenge you should be driven by the love of it and not by money.

- Success is never final. Everyone will experience failure but successful people are those who best recover from failure and disappointment. Failure is never fatal. There is always the hope of another success and another goal to strive for and achieve.

CHAPTER ELEVEN

CONSISTENCY

'Victory is what happens when 10,000 hours of preparation meet with one moment of opportunity.' **UNKNOWN**

'The lower the lows, the higher the highs.' **SCOTT VOLKERS**

People always wonder how I consistently win. But I'm rarely happy with most of my swims and can always see areas of improvement. Even though I'm an Olympic, World and Commonwealth Games champion I know I'm far from perfect and I'm still looking for the perfect race. Swimmers have comparatively few chances of making their mark. Olympic and Commonwealth Games and World Championships are only held every four years. If you make a mistake then there is a long waiting period to rectify the result. So I never take reaching the top dais for granted.

1998 was an amazing year for me. I claimed four medals at the World Championships–a gold, a silver and two bronze. I then won four individual finals at the National Championships to bring my tally to 30 titles. At the Commonwealth Games I stood on the dais eight times–six times as gold medallist and twice as silver medallist. Probably to the average person it seemed a great effort but I know there are a string of faults I have to finetune to be ready for the 2000 Olympics.

Most people only see the triumphs and glory of sports champions and not the hard slog in training, especially when nothing goes right. I'm sure most people would be surprised at how many shocking training sessions I've had. My worst training period came after my 1998 success. It brought me down to earth very quickly from my incredible high. I made the mistake of over-training when I returned from my break after the Commonwealth Games. It was too much too soon and my body broke down. I felt very lethargic and powerless and could barely lift my arms above the water.

It was especially hard when my bad training form dragged on for four weeks into January 1999. I knew I hadn't suddenly lost my fitness overnight and my coach Scott Volkers kept repeating that I would not be this slow forever. It was a matter of working through it. Only a few weeks before I had won my tenth Commonwealth Games gold medal in Kuala Lumpur but here in training I could not pass one swimmer. Even my husband Cliff was overtaking me, which had never happened before. It was incredibly frustrating for someone so used to accelerating past the world's best.

I was so close to giving up in training on several occasions. To help me get through, Scott would say, 'the lower the low, the higher the high'. Scott was right because after persevering and remaining positive during my lengthy low I finally rebounded and surprised myself with a world short-course record in the 200m butterfly and three national titles in February and March 1999.

In a handful of weeks I had experienced the highs of competition success to the lows of training woes and then back to a high. Lows keep you down to earth and make the highs even more satisfying. I realised neither highs nor lows are permanent but it is important to treat both with the constant approach of hard work. Everybody makes mistakes and experiences lows but it is the people who learn from them who become consistent achievers.

THE 1998 WORLD CHAMPIONSHIPS IN PERTH

Performing after success

Success brings the expectation you will win again. You can not control outside pressure but you can control how it affects you. When the level of expectation and pressure becomes too much then return to the simple formula of what and why you want to achieve.

Everyone has a goal they dream for years of achieving, be it attaining a certain job, becoming a millionaire, owning your own home or a sports achievement. My long-time aspiration was to win an Olympic gold medal but once that goal became a reality at 23 years of age it brought a different proposition. The title of Olympic champion carries high expectation. After my

Atlanta success I felt that I was expected to win all the time. It was probably more the pressure I was putting on myself than outside influences. I had a particularly difficult time the year after my Olympic success in 1997. Things change once you become the rabbit that everyone is chasing. Once I won the Olympic gold medal I became the one person everyone wanted to beat. Because I was seen as the measuring stick, everyone else was motivated to swim their best against me. I found the more I won, the more success I had to defend and the greater the pressure.

The first races after I won the Olympic gold medal were a couple of fairly low-key meets in the United States. I didn't swim well in those meets because I was so distracted by the pressure and expectation. My problems culminated at the 1997 Pan Pacific championships in Japan. The Pan Pacs was my first major international competition after Atlanta. I felt as the Olympic champion I should at least win the Pan Pacs because everything else was a step down from the Olympics. In the 200m butterfly I panicked. I fell back to my old bad habits and became worried about fast-starting American swimmer Misty Hyman. I tightened up in the race and somehow managed to hold on for a win even though I was a long way from my best.

By early 1998 I realised things were not right. I thought to myself, 'What am I doing?' I didn't want to get an ulcer every time I competed. I wanted to enjoy swimming again but instead it was taking so much energy and strength to defend my success. Then I realised I had already met my own expectations when I achieved my ultimate goal, an Olympic gold medal. Everything else was a bonus. Because I had already proved I could win at the highest level, I no longer had a reason to feel pressure. I entered the 1998 world championships in January in Perth relaxed, no longer burdened by pressure to succeed, which helped me win the 200m butterfly title.

The right team balance

Whether in business, sport or socially a team will not be successful until it is balanced with the right blend of youth and experience. Veterans know how to win which complements the infectious enthusiasm and confidence of youth. The most successful combinations have a mixture of both which will only help to boost team spirit.

It's amazing how when people around you win, you start believing you can also do well. It's always important to have self-motivation but there's no doubt a great team spirit contributes to success. At the Atlanta Olympics losing became contagious and there was not a great team balance but at the 1998 World Championships the youth and veterans in the team clicked. When in the crowd members of the swimming team wore Australian masks, waved Australian flags and made an effort to stay and cheer their team-mates. A big factor which lifts team spirit is when Australia has success on the first day of competitions such as when Michael Klim won the 200m freestyle at the world championships. It's amazing how winning can be infectious.

Leading into the World Championships there were several young swimmers such as Klim, Ian Thorpe, Grant Hackett, Geoff Huegill and Rebecca Creedy who were hungry and confident. It was a different environment to when I first made the Australian team when few believed they could be the best in the world. Now these young swimmers take it for granted that if you train hard you can be world champion. Klim, Hackett, Thorpe, Huegill and Creedy all won medals at the World Championships despite their inexperience at big-time racing. The younger swimmers have kept us more mature swimmers on our toes and have helped to re-ignite our excitement at competing for Australia. Us older swimmers have provided experience and stability. The competition between young and old helps everyone to swim faster which will only continue to boost team spirit.

THE 1998 COMMONWEALTH GAMES IN KUALA LUMPUR

Rebounding from setbacks

Everyone has setbacks which can be disappointing and frustrating. The only way to rebound quickly is with a positive attitude and a willingness to learn. It is important you only allow setbacks to slow you down temporarily and not permanently damage your will or ability to win.

Prior to the 1998 Commonwealth Games I had already overcome a major setback: just before the national titles (which doubled as the Commonwealth Games trials) in Melbourne earlier in the year I was informed I was close to breaking Frank Beaurepaire's record of 29 national titles. After that there was rarely a time the record was not mentioned. Under intense pressure and hype, I had to win four of the five individual events I raced including my last event, the 200m butterfly.

It was one of my biggest thrills when I thought I had broken the record. The memory is still so clear: the announcement of my successful attempt at the pool; stepping up onto the dais; everyone standing up and applauding; receiving the flowers and the medal; and bursting into tears with all the emotion. I am never emotional on the dais, not even when I won the gold medal in Atlanta, but I broke that tradition and cried at the National Titles. It was such a special moment.

I was devastated when I heard the news a few days later that Beaurepaire had won four more titles and therefore I had not broken the record. I realised the only way I could recover quickly from the disappointment was to view it positively. I now think of the night as a 'thank you' from the public and swimming community. So many former swimmers say that when they left the Australian team no one ever sent them a letter thanking them for their years of contribution. So even though I had not yet broken Beaurepaire's record I felt that it was my 'thank you' and no one could take away my memories of that special night.

I also viewed the Beaurepaire experience as an ideal dress rehearsal for the pressure I would have to withstand at Kuala Lumpur with my attempt at eclipsing Michael Wenden's record of nine Commonwealth Games gold medals. In an almost similar scenario to the trials I had to win the 200m butterfly on the final day at Kuala Lumpur to become the most successful Commonwealth Games athlete of all time with ten gold medals. It was my only chance at the record because it was my last Commonwealth Games. But I had learnt from the Beaurepaire experience and I knew the strong focus required to compete under so much pressure. Triumphing under pressure once, gives you the confidence you can do it again. I not only won but I swam a personal best time of 2:06.6, the second fastest 200m butterfly time in history. Achieving the Beaurepaire and Wenden records in the public spotlight will be great practice for the 2000 Olympics where I'm sure I will face the most pressure I've ever experienced. By putting positive twists on the disappointment at the trials, I was able to quickly recover and put all my energy and knowledge into my Commonwealth Games campaign and future performances.

Prepared for all conditions

It is impossible to control all conditions of an event but you can prepare for the things you know about. Research the conditions and know what to expect and what adjustments would need to be made for things such as weather and food. Failure to research and adequately adjust to all conditions could prove costly.

Five minutes before my 200m freestyle heat swim at the 1998 Commonwealth Games in Kuala Lumpur I fainted. I believe it was largely due to my failure to adjust to the conditions. Kuala Lumpur is extremely hot and humid. I had a gastric illness and I was not adequately keeping up my fluid intake of several litres a day and I'm sure drinking coffee before my races would not have helped this. I had just completed a fantastic warm-up session and then wrapped myself in a hot Australian track suit, which made the situation even worse. By the time I exited the change rooms people said I looked as white as a sheet. I had just walked into the marshalling area and then everything started caving in. There were big sails on the roof and I remember feeling they were coming down on me. I started seeing stars and had to sit down. I couldn't get enough air, I felt claustrophobic even though it was an outdoor pool. I remember everything closing down and I couldn't breathe. I was dehydrated and had hypoglycaemia. A doctor was called and I had a drink, a Panadol and something to eat which made me feel better.

This happened five minutes before the scheduled start of the heat swims on the second day of competition and I was in the second race. There is no doubt I would have been forced to pull out but I was lucky. In one of only two occasions the swimming started late when it was delayed for about 30 minutes. I somehow managed to complete my heat swim and qualify for the 200m freestyle final. I knew I had to hold it together, ignore my exhaustion and I would be all right for the final. I won the 200m freestyle final but in a slow time. The incident meant I was tired and not quite at my best for the next couple of days. Before the Games, Scott had believed I was in the form to swim personal bests in all my races. Petria Thomas was swimming well and deserved to win the 100m butterfly but I can not expect to produce a peak performance when I didn't adequately prepare for Kuala Lumpur. It was my fault. I had misjudged the heat and humidity and because of that I was unable to perform at my best.

You can not wrap yourself in cotton wool but make sure you are prepared and ready to perform at your peak. I'm determined not to be under-prepared again especially for the 2000 Olympics and this time I will do my homework and be ready for all conditions.

CHAPTER
FOCUS

- It is the lows which make the highs so satisfying. Success comes by treating both the lows and highs with the same consistent approach.

- A team will not be successful until it is balanced with the right blend of youth and experience.

- Setbacks should only slow you down temporarily and not permanently damage your will or ability to win.

- It is impossible to control all conditions of an event but prepare for the things you can.

CHAPTER TWELVE

WINNING

'If you come expecting an argument, you will end up in a battle. Be prepared for a battle every time.' **SCOTT VOLKERS**

'It's like a title fight for the heavyweight championship of the world and that was only the first round. You have to get back up for round two.' **GANARDI TOURETSKY**

I **was in the middle of delivering a speech at a business lunch when a weird feeling came over me.** I suddenly felt like I was a freak show. People wanted to listen to me, touch me, have me autograph their programmes and to be photographed with me. I thought, 'What am I doing here?'. Ever since July 1996 when I won a gold medal in Atlanta, I've been known publicly, but the level of recognition and interest has increased ten-fold since the 1998 Commonwealth Games. I'm a regular guest at functions and I still can't believe all these people want to hear me speak.

The shopping centre visits are probably the most surreal experiences. All these people, mainly kids, are screaming for you. It's a weird sensation to be the focus of such a public frenzy. Sometimes it can feel as though I'm part of a strange exhibition, like, 'Let's go and see the three-legged lady'. I suppose the achievements of sports stars are so public. I used to feel daunted by all the attention but now I feel visiting shopping centres and speaking to people are things I can do to give back to the community. I now feel that swimming up and down a pool as fast as I can has a purpose. I'm providing entertainment for people, like going to the movies. But I don't get carried away with fame. I think people were surprised at my shopping centre visits when I carried my eight-medal Commonwealth Games haul in a mundane plastic shopping bag.

I received more than 10,000 faxes and thousands of letters after the Commonwealth Games and I'm still writing back to people. Mum is helping because of the number of letters. There was one day she opened so many envelopes that her hands bled. I suppose winning six gold medals and a record total of ten was well documented. Personally I feel winning one Olympic gold medal is still better than winning six at the Commonwealth Games. It seemed more people saw my Commonwealth Games swims than my Olympic gold medal success probably because it was on prime time television. The night I won my 200m butterfly 605,000 south-east Queenslanders were watching as the third most popular show of the year.

The atmosphere in Kuala Lumpur was excellent, especially at the closing ceremony. In a career highlight I was chosen to carry the Australian flag. It was amazing and the best part was that I was allowed to keep the flag which I proudly display at home. It was such an honour to represent my country like that. It took my breath away marching out into the packed stadium but the fun really started when the official part was over. I took off my shoes and grabbed my flag and kept running around the stadium with everyone else. 1998 was a big year in every way. It was an emotional and exciting year after success in the pool but more importantly I married Cliff Fairley. I wanted to have a wedding like a normal person but everything seemed to get out of control with publicity. I suppose people don't know much about my personal side and everyone was interested. But it all worked out in the end.

Athletes have so much pressure to deal with these days. It can scare anyone when you start thinking about the 'what ifs' and all the ramifications of success and failure. That is why I keep my focus on swimming rather than outside the pool. I'm aware that the public only like winners and by training hard I continue to win. It is why I appreciate training because it is where I can be myself away from all the hype and pressure. It's like my office. As Cliff always says to me, I'm getting paid to keep fit for a living. My matter-of-fact approach to swimming as my job has helped me to avoid becoming big-headed. It is how I keep choosing to win. Some people work on computers all day, others serve behind shop counters or mow lawns. I concentrate on swimming well.

ACHIEVING THE ZONE

I was in my tenth year of international competition when at the 1998 Commonwealth Games I finally achieved the experience of entering the hallowed 'zone' in competition. It was in the 200m butterfly when I swam a personal best 2:06.6, only 0.64 of a second slower than Mary T. Meagher's 1981 record. I've heard other athletes talking about being in the zone; I've read about their experiences in books and magazines such as tennis players who feel like the ball is on a piece of string and they can perfectly place it; and I've seen other swimmers perform while in the zone. But I had never experienced it myself until now. Nothing prepared me for the experience. I had felt good in races before but not like this.

It was a weird feeling because I felt like I was in another world. I didn't feel much pain which is unusual, even in the last lap when I had a lot of energy left. I felt strong but also remarkably light. Every time I gripped the water it was an awesome grip and I easily moved through it. The race was going so fast and I was concentrating so hard but I was thinking about nothing. Even at the 1996 Olympic Games in the 200m butterfly my mind was wandering but here I had total focus–not one stray thought. Winning the Olympics is still my career highlight but I've never been more excited than after my 200m butterfly at the Commonwealth Games because of the time I made. I could not believe that I swam that fast because it felt so easy. It was a huge breakthrough and it has renewed my confidence and motivation to break Meagher's record.

Maybe I'm a slow learner but it's amazing how it has taken me so long to enter the zone. Then, within six months of the Commonwealth Games, I produced another zone swim, when I broke Meagher's 18-year-old short-course 200m butterfly record. I've realised for me to swim a world record I have to be in the zone. And now I've been there twice I know I can repeat that experience. I have identified five factors behind entering the zone. Basically it is about being in total physical and mental focus, something which is essential for anyone wanting to achieve success in any field.

1 Physical zone

I realised it was no coincidence that I achieved my two best swims when I was the fittest I've ever been. I competed in the 400m freestyle for the first time in 1998. But ironically swimming it had more to do with the training required for the 400m freestyle than actually racing the event. I swam a heap of kilometres before the Commonwealth Games. I averaged 42 kilometres a week in training before the Olympic Games in Atlanta. But leading to Kuala Lumpur it went to 70 kilometres a week and I registered a peak of 90 kilometres one week. I swam 435 kilometres over a six week period which was incredible for me and very tiring. I was not performing exceptionally in training, just consistently ploughing through the kilometres, but I still enjoyed the training change.

I felt so much fitter but more importantly all those sessions gave me the confidence when I stepped up onto the blocks at the Commonwealth Games. I knew I would have something in reserve for the last 50m in the 200m butterfly even though I had swum 14 races in six days. I was also confident after finetuning my stroke with assistant coach Stephan Widmar who made some technical changes. Training for the 400m freestyle, even though I'm unlikely to ever swim it again, will continue to 2000 as part of a special Olympic plan. It should really help my 200m butterfly in Sydney with three years of heavy training behind me. By September 2000 I plan to be the fittest I've ever been and with all physical bases covered it can only help me reach the zone again.

2 Mental zone

Getting my head in the right mental zone was behind my Commonwealth Games success. There was potential to let distractions affect me, especially with my highly publicised attempt to break Michael Wenden's record of nine gold medals. During my 200m butterfly final warm-up an Australian team official asked me in the middle of the session how many Commonwealth Games gold medals I had won. I should have been strong enough not to let something like that distract me but I did. I was swimming terribly, I was tense and my mind was everywhere. I started thinking about breaking the Wenden record and winning ten gold medals instead of what I needed to do to win.

I did one more warm-up lap and Scott pulled me out of the pool and spoke to me. The moment is etched so clearly in my mind. There could have been others swimming in the pool or around the deck but because I was listening so intently I did not notice another soul. Scott talked to me for about ten minutes in a forceful tone. Scott said later he could see straight into my eyes that I was taking it in and that I was focused. But I don't think even Scott expected me to unleash such a swim. I was in the zone. I never thought about times, medals, records or my opposition.

When I dived in I pretended there were curtains in between the lane ropes blacking out the other lanes. Scott and I had not talked about times but only feelings like swimming the first 50 m butterfly 'easy', building the second and third 50 metres and then trying not to go too fast in the fourth. When you try too hard that is when you can become unstuck. I was so focused that I did not know where any other swimmer was in the race. I only saw the race recently on television at a function and I had no idea that Petria had stuck with me for the first 100 metres. If I had known that I may have panicked but instead I had my curtains up and every other swimmer was blocked out. Now my aim is to achieve the mental zone for every race leading to the 2000 Olympics.

3 Always be prepared

You can only achieve the zone if you are fully prepared. I under-estimated my opposition at my first European World Cup meet in Glasgow in February 1999. I arrived not expecting strong competition with most key contenders absent such as Petria Thomas and Danish swimmer Mette Jacobsen. I assumed I would win. I paid for my poor preparation because during the race I panicked when I realised I was not race-ready. German swimmer Katrin Jaeke, whom I had beaten comfortably in Sydney and Hobart the month before, pushed me all the way and I only narrowly held onto victory. I was simply not prepared and I realised then if I dropped off even a small percentage then I would get beaten. Scott came up with the saying that I came in expecting an argument and ended up in a battle. He says I should be prepared for a battle every time. I came prepared for my next two meetings, Malmo, Sweden, and Paris, France, where I swam a new world record and the third fastest time in history. The scare in Glasgow provided the wake-up call I needed for every upcoming race. I now realise it is when I'm ready for a fight that I increase my chances of reaching the zone and winning.

4 Never have limitations

The short-course world record I set in Malmo, Sweden, made me realise never to carry limits or doubts into a race because if I had I would not have won or set the new mark. Everything was against me and I could have easily discarded myself a chance at setting a world record. I had painful infected wisdom teeth; I had a disrupted training lead-up; I had a terrible race warm-up; I had swum poorly in Glasgow; and I had struggled in my 100m butterfly the day before. Instead I never limited my expectations no matter how dire my preparation and form seemed to be.

I was shocked when I looked at the time in Malmo. I don't know what time I was expecting but I wasn't expecting a 2:05:65 swim. I shaved .3 second off a world record which had stood since January 2, 1981–the oldest swimming world record, male or female, long course or short, in the book. I actually swam the first 100 metres in the 200m race faster than my individual 100m butterfly race. I had not thought about times before the race because setting yourself splits in a race or a time you want to achieve automatically creates limits and expectation.

The Malmo race has changed how I think and prepare for races. It would have been easy to fall into the trap of thinking I had no chance. But when I was in the zone I had been so focused I did not let anything worry me. Before the World Cup in Hobart in January everyone was talking about the world record and I said to Scott there was no way I could break it because I didn't consider I was swimming well enough. But I've realised anything is possible after improving by three seconds in three days between the Glasgow and Malmo races. I will not doubt myself in any situation again.

5 Recreating the zone

The most exciting aspect of being in the zone is the thought of returning. I realise it's important not to bask in the success of achieving it but to analyse and re-analyse every part of the race to make sure it happens again. After the Commonwealth Games Scott and I talked about the race several times. He said it was important to understand how I achieved the zone. Kuala Lumpur and Malmo had similarities: not thinking about times; refocusing before both swims; and a tremendous focus which overcame terrible race-warm-ups and illness. In Malmo I was on antibiotics for an inflamed jaw because I had infected wisdom teeth which were very painful. I had a sore lower back during my Commonwealth Games swim which gave me pins and needles and was painful when I tumble turned.

The only way to recreate the zone experience is by practice. It's good to swim a lot of races because they provide the best form of practice. Each time I swim a race I become more experienced at achieving a total focus and reaching the zone whether the race is a local meet or an international competition. So by the time I stand on the blocks at the 2000 Olympics I will be on autopilot. I won't be distracted and looking around thinking that this is my last ever race. I won't be feeling the pressure of competing in Australia and knowing everyone is watching and expecting me to win. I can dive in and just keep doing what I've been doing in the dozens of previous races.

Scott always likes to repeat the remark Ganardi Touretsky made after Michael Klim broke the 100m butterfly world record after swimming 70m in a false start at the 1997 national titles in Brisbane: 'It's like a title fight for the heavyweight championship of the world and that was only the first round. You have to get back up for round two.'

I believe I've got more rounds remaining and I'm not finished yet.

CHAPTER
FOCUS

- Achieving the zone is about total mental and physical focus and a thorough preparation.

- Never limit your expectations, no matter how dire your preparation and form seem to be, because you may surprise yourself.

- The most exciting aspect of being in the zone is the thought of returning. It's important not to bask in the success of achieving it but to analyse and re-analyse to make sure it happens again.

THE FIVE STEPS IN CHOOSING TO WIN

Step One: Balance–The first step to success because without balance in your life it's impossible to find a stable platform on which to build your dreams and keep your ego down to earth.

Step Two: Hard Work and Perseverance–No dream can be turned into reality without a high work ethic and perseverance, which comes from finding enjoyment and hunger in watching each layer form.

Step Three: Learn and Improve–Learn from experiences and people around you. The best goal you can have is improvement which, no matter how big or small, always raises you to the next level.

Step Four: Self-focus–The fastest way to victory is a rock-solid self-focus to keep out the distractions which will destabilise your tower of goals.

Step Five: Self-belief–Finally, you cannot overcome your toughest obstacles and choose to win until you believe you can.

Swimming Career Highlights

As at April 1999

1989: PAN PACIFIC TITLES (Tokyo, Japan) – sixth in 100m butterfly (1:01.57), sixth in 100m freestyle (57.63), eighth in 200m freestyle (2:04.75) and fourth in four by 100m and 200m freestyle relays.

1990: COMMONWEALTH GAMES (Auckland, New Zealand) – SILVER in 100m butterfly (1:01.03) and GOLD in four by 100m freestyle relay.

1991: WORLD CHAMPIONSHIPS (Perth, Australia) – fifth in 100m butterfly (Commonwealth record – 1:00.54), first in B final 100m freestyle (Commonwealth record – 56.20) and SILVER in the four by 100m medley relay (Nicole Stevensen, Lindley Frame and Karen Van Wirnum).

PAN PACIFIC TITLES (Edmonton, Canada) – GOLD in 100m butterfly (Commonwealth record – 59.93), BRONZE in 100m freestyle (56.12), SILVER in 100m medley relay, BRONZE in four by 200m freestyle relay, and BRONZE in four by 100m freestyle relay.

1992: OLYMPIC GAMES (Barcelona, Spain) – BRONZE in 200m butterfly (Commonwealth record – 2:09.08), fifth in 100m butterfly (Commonwealth record – 59.69), third in B final in 200m freestyle (2:00.89), seventh in B final in 100m freestyle (56.65) and fifth in four by 100m medley relay.

1993: PAN PACIFIC TITLES (Kobe, Japan) – SILVER in 100m freestyle (Commonwealth record – 55.80), SILVER in 100m butterfly (59.86), fifth in 200m freestyle (2:01.05), SILVER in four by 100m freestyle relay, SILVER in four by 200m freestyle relay, and

5

SILVER in four by 100m medley relay.

WORLD SHORTCOURSE TITLES (Madrid, Spain) – GOLD in 100m butterfly (59.19), SILVER in 200m butterfly (2:09.08), SILVER in 200m freestyle (1:57.1), SILVER in four by 200m freestyle relay, SILVER in four by 100m freestyle relay and SILVER in four by 100m medley relay.

1994: COMMONWEALTH GAMES (Victoria, Canada) – GOLD in 200m freestyle (2:00.86), GOLD in 200m butterfly (2:09.97), SILVER in 100m butterfly (1:00.24), GOLD in four by 200m freestyle relay and SILVER in four by 100m freestyle relay.

WORLD CHAMPIONSHIPS (Rome, Italy) – BRONZE in 100m butterfly (1:00.11), BRONZE in 200m butterfly (2:09.57), sixth in 200m freestyle (2:00.46), fourth in four by 200m freestyle relay, fourth in four by 100m medley relay and fourth in four by 100m freestyle relay.

1995: PAN PACIFIC TITLES (Atlanta, United States) – GOLD in 200m butterfly (Commonwealth record – 2:07.29), GOLD in 100m butterfly (Commonwealth record – 59.58), GOLD in four by 100m medley relay, SILVER in four by 100m freestyle relay and SILVER in four by 200m medley relay.

WORLD SHORTCOURSE TITLES (Rio de Janeiro, Brazil) – GOLD in 200m butterfly (2:06.18), SILVER in 100m butterfly (58:69), SILVER in 200m freestyle (1:56.47), GOLD in four by 100m medley relay, SILVER in four by 100m freestyle relay and BRONZE in four by 200m freestyle relay.

1996: OLYMPIC GAMES (Atlanta, United States) – GOLD in 200m butterfly (2:07.76), fifth in 100m butterfly (1:00.17), fifth in 200m freestyle (1:59.87), SILVER in four by 100m medley relay, BRONZE in four by 200m freestyle relay and sixth in four by 100m freestyle relay.

1997: PAN PACIFIC TITLES (Fukoka, Japan) – GOLD in 200m butterfly (2:08.59), fifth in 100m butterfly (1:00.40), fifth in 100m freestyle (56.36), SILVER in four by 100m medley relay, BRONZE in four by 100m freestyle relay, BRONZE in four by 200m freestyle relay.

1998: WORLD CHAMPIONSHIPS (Perth, Australia) – GOLD in 200m butterfly (2:07.93), fifth in 100m butterfly (59.27), sixth in 200m freestyle (2:00.33), SILVER in four by 100m medley relay, BRONZE in four by 100m freestyle relay, BRONZE in four by 200m freestyle relay.

COMMONWEALTH GAMES (Kuala Lumpur, Malaysia) – GOLD in 200m butterfly (2:06.6), GOLD in 200m freestyle (2:00.24), GOLD in 400m freestyle (4:12.39), SILVER in 100m butterfly (59.61), SILVER in 100m freestyle (55.58), GOLD in four by 100m medley relay, GOLD in four by 100m freestyle relay, GOLD in four by 200m freestyle relay.

TOTAL medal count: 20 gold, 24 silver and 12 bronze

WORLD NUMBER ONE RANKING
200m butterfly (1995–98)
100m butterfly (1995)

WORLD ALL-TIME TOP RANKING
200m butterfly
1. 2:05.96 Mary T. Meagher, USA Brown Deer 13-08-81
2. 2:06.6 Susie O'Neill, AUS Kuala Lumpur 17-09-98
200m butterfly (short-course)

1. 2:05.37 Susie O'Neill, AUS Malmo 18-2-99
100m butterfly
17. 59.27 Susie O'Neill, AUS Perth 15-01-98
200m freestyle
20. 1:59.11 Susie O'Neill, AUS Brisbane 23-03-99

AUSTRALIAN ALL-TIME TOP RANKING
100m freestyle
1. 55.58 Susie O'Neill, Kuala Lumpur 12-09-98
200m freestyle
1. 1:59.11 Susie O'Neill, Brisbane 23-03-99
100m butterfly
1. 58.97 Petria Thomas, Perth 15-01-98
2. 59.27 Susie O'Neill, Perth 15-01-98
200m butterfly
1. 2:06.6 Susie O'Neill, Kuala Lumpur 17-09-98

AWARDS
Order of Australian Medal – OAM (1997)
Female Olympian of the Year (1996)
Australian Swimmer of the Year (1995, '96)
Australian Freestyle Sprinter of the Year (1991, '98)
Australian Butterflyer/female Butterflyer of the Year (1991–98)
Australian MLC Young Achiever of the Year (1993)
Australian Sportswoman of the Year (1996, '98)
Queensland Sportswoman of the Year (1992, '96, '98)
Queensland Sportsperson of the Year (1996)
Queensland Young Achiever of the Year (1996)
People's Choice, Australia's most popular sportswoman (1998)
(All above information correct as at April, 1999)